eBay®
Home Run

Also by Lynn A. Dralle:

The 3rd 100 Best Things I've Sold on eBay...Ka-Ching!
2007

The Unofficial Guide to Making Money on eBay
John Wiley & Sons, Inc., 2006

More 100 Best Things I've Sold on eBay
Money Making Madness
June 2006

How to Sell Antiques and Collectibles on eBay...
and Make a Fortune!
with Dennis Prince; McGraw Hill, 2005

The 100 Best Things I've Sold on eBay
2004

I Sell on eBay Tracking Binder
1999

I Buy on eBay Tracking Binder
1999

The Unauthorized Beanie Baby Guide
with Lee Dralle; Scholastic, 1998

The Book of Beanie Babies
with Lee Dralle; AKA, 1998

The **4**th **100 Best**
Things I've Sold on

eBay®
Home Run

My Story Continues
by The Queen of Auctions
Lynn A. Dralle

"4 Bases Makes a Home Run"
"4 100 Best Books makes a
Series"

All Aboard, Inc.

Preface

As I write this new book in my series, I am sitting in my office in Palm Desert, CA, thinking how different this book is starting out than *The 3rd 100 Best*.

The 3rd 100 Best book I began writing on a balcony in the Grand Caymans enjoying a well earned vacation.

This book begins with the world seeing a bleak economic outlook, more foreclosures than ever in history and people losing their jobs left and right. Fortunately, for those of us who sell on eBay—eBay is still a home run.

2008 was my personal best year ever selling on eBay ($147,000, not including any of my books or other eBay learning products), and although this book doesn't include any single "home run" sales (single items that sell for a lot of money, $1,000 plus, and actually bring in a profit—please see story #36 to see what I mean!), what you will see in this book is that it is the day-to-day single sales for $25 to $300 that add up to make eBay an overall home run.

I make my living selling A LOT of $10 items. eBay is still and always will be a numbers game. Don't forget that.

In tough economic times, people tend to hold more garage sales and also tend to shop for bargains. eBay is the perfect fit for what is happening to the world. I encourage you to jump in and test the eBay waters. If you are already in, I wish you incredible success and lots of home runs!

Lynn

P.S. Once again my grandmother is the person who inspired me to follow in her footsteps, write these books, teach others to be just as successful as I am (or even more so), and who I miss every day. The 4th book in this series shows just how strong her influence and spirit were because they are still shining through. Thank you for reading this!

eBay with
♡ Heart
Lynn

vi

First Edition 2009

ISBN-10: 0-9768393-2-6
ISBN-13: 978-0-9768393-2-3

For more information write:

All Aboard, Inc.
P.O. Box 14103
Palm Desert, CA 92255

Lynn@TheQueenofAuctions.com
www.TheQueenofAuctions.com

Designed by: Lee Dralle (LADralle.com), Becky Raney
and Lynn A. Dralle
Edited by: Susan Thornberg

Printed in the United States of America
Print & Copy Factory
4055 Irongate Road
Bellingham, WA 98226
www.printcopyfactory.com

This book is dedicated to
Houston and Indiana

I love you two
and your
amazingly positive spirits.

You are such great
kids and you keep
me motivated and
laughing all the time.

I am so proud of you
both!

Acknowledgments

My greatest thanks to:
Cheryl Leaf
Lee Dralle
Susan Thornberg
Becky and Larry Raney
Houston and Indiana
Sharon Chase
Wayne and Sue Dralle
Kristin Dralle
Peter Gineris
Maureen Arcand
Juliette Capretta
Carmen & Jason Badham
Melanie Souve
Deborah Fisher
eBay Boot Camp Graduates
My Awesome Queen's Court Members
My eBay students
eBay
Readers of my books and ezine
AND all our great eBay customers!

Contents

Introduction

The 4th 100 Best *Home Run*

Afterword

Introduction

Grandma

My grandma was an amazing lady. Not only did she run an antiques store for over 50 years, but she had a blast doing it. Everyone around her could feel the passion and joy she got out of doing what she loved—buying and sometimes selling her antiques. She said that she never regretted buying an antique or a piece of real estate, but she did regret selling them.

One of her long time customers, Billie Ershig, was in one day and said to me, "I don't think your grandma cares if she ever sells anything." I laughed, because it was kind of true. However, my grandmother loved to make money. She was very skilled at running her business and was super successful over the years.

She passed along to me a very strong work ethic, but also the conviction that work could and SHOULD be fun. My grandmother always made me feel special and she made me believe that I could do and be anything. My parents look at me sometimes as I plug away and ask, "Why don't you ever give up?" Give up? That is NOT an option.

My grandma really started dabbling in antiques quite a few years before she opened her antiques store. The story goes that when they lived at 2724 Victor Street in a house my grandfather built (he was an architect), she started stockpiling antiques in the basement.

At the time, my grandmother was working at Haskell's Plumbing as a bookkeeper, and almost every weekend she, my grandfather, and my mother went to British Columbia to buy antiques (Highway 99 was lined with antique stores). Then they would go to a hockey game, which was a reward for my grandpa, who loved hockey but would get bored silly waiting for my grandma to finish her antique shopping. My kids feel the same way when I drag them out to garage sales!

By the way, my grandmother never EVER went to a garage sale, so the fact that I depend on them for my living still feels strange to me. But the world is constantly changing, and garage sales rock...as you will see.

In the early days of her business, my grandma ran an ad in the Bellingham newspaper letting people know that she had antiques to sell. Martha, who eventually became my grandmother's best friend, answered one ad and came by bus to see what my grandma had on hand. My mom still remembers seeing Martha walk up the front sidewalk. My grandmother was only 33 years old and had already found her passion.

A few years later as my mom was walking to school, she found a house for sale on old Highway 99 (which eventually became NW Avenue). My grandma was overjoyed and immediately bought the property. The year was 1949; my mom was in junior high, and my grandmother opened her store in 1950 in a small front section of the living room.

The rest is history. The shop was open for business for the next 52 years. I am proud of my grandmother for being a pioneer as a woman in business and miss her every day.

eBay

My grandmother fell and broke her hip in January of 1993. By April of 1993, my Los Angeles condo was sold, and I had moved back to Bellingham to get her out of the nursing home, take care of her, and run her business. It was an incredible experience for me. As an adult, I got to spend quality time with my greatest mentor and learn on a minute-by-minute basis. I learned not only about antiques and running a business, but about how to be a good, kind, and generous soul.

I also got married and had two babies that my grandmother got to hold and kiss (and in some instances they kissed her back). She loved Houston and Indiana from the moment she saw them—no questions asked.

When my grandmother got sick again in 1999 with a lung illness that had nothing to do with smoking (she had never smoked) or cancer (she had battled and survived cancer while I was in high school), we had to put her into a nursing home. It was an incredibly hard decision. But all of a sudden we needed to raise a lot of money to pay for her care.

Enter eBay. We had to just jump in, and that was hard back in 1999. I had owned a user ID on eBay since September 11, 1998 (ironically, my parents' wedding day was September 11) and had dabbled sporadically in both buying and selling—but now it was serious.

We started our eBay business with all of my grandmother's inventory, so right off the bat we were selling $20,000 a month. Once I got started selling, I couldn't stop. It was addict-ing. It is like gambling, without the risk of losing. I am hooked. I still list at least 100 new items each week on eBay, and sometimes 200 each week (except for this week that I am finishing this book—I only have sixteen items listed and I am freaking out!).

My grandmother passed away on August 2, 2000. My brother was with her and when he called me to tell me of her passing, I was holding Indy (who was then 1 1/2) in my arms; she had a fever. I almost felt like my grandmother's fighting spirit was transferred to my daughter. It was incredibly sad.

We decided to close the store after two years of liquidating the remaining merchandise. We closed the doors of my grandmother's brick-and-mortar store exactly two years to the day after she died. It was Friday, August 2nd, 2002.

By October of 2002, I had divorced and moved my kids back to Southern California. eBay gave us the option of living anywhere we wanted to.

The 100 Best Things I've Sold on eBay

In April of 2003, about six months after arriving in California, I decided I wanted to write a book honoring my grandmother. I started writing it focusing on the hundred most important things I had learned from her, but it was slow going.

In September of 2003, I was teaching a class about eBay for The Learning Annex in Los Angeles. I told a story about an Edwardian mourning case that I'd sold earlier in the year (see #74 in *The 100 Best Things I've Sold on eBay)*. One of the women in the class yelled out, "That story gave me goosebumps!" My stories were her favorite part of the entire three-hour class. Wow! I realized that I had lots of stories to tell about my eBay successes (and failures). For failures in this book, please see story #36 for my biggest failure EVER!

After hearing my student's "goosebumps" comment, I realized that I could combine my eBay stories and my grandmother's lessons into a single book. I could use my eBay experiences as a framework for my grandmother's story—the lessons she taught me, the stories she told, the life she lived. I was excited! When I started writing that book, I couldn't stop!

That book is *The 100 Best Things I've Sold on eBay,* and it is the first in this series. Almost every day I get an email from someone who has read *The 100 Best,* and they tell me what an inspiration it has been to them. That warms my heart.

More 100 Best Things I've Sold on eBay—Money Making Madness

In 2006 I had acquired another 100 great items for a book, and I started writing *Money Making Madness.* The two years in between books had taught me a lot! I found that I had to re-learn much of what I had been taught in the antiques store.

Things that would sell in our shop in Bellingham, Washington, didn't always bring much on eBay, if they sold at all. On the flip side, things that I wouldn't ever have considered stocking in our store sold for big bucks on eBay—items such as empty vintage cereal boxes, skateboards, and telephone line insulators. *The 100 Best* books give me the opportunity to share many of the lessons I've learned with readers in a fun and entertaining format.

Money Making Madness, the second book in this series, contains stories about more items that I actually had to go out and buy than the first *100 Best* book does. The items weren't just handed to me by my grandmother. That is one reason the second book is so fun.

I was scared at first to leave the shop and see if I really could make a living by going to garage sales. I am happy to report that my new business model is working out incredibly well for me. In fact, the items that have brought in the most money on eBay are not those that I inherited, but things I bought at garage and estate sales for $2 to $20.

The 3rd 100 Best Things I've Sold on eBay—Ka-Ching!

Money Making Madness ended with a story about a toaster that I sold on May 8, 2005. So, in early 2007 I realized that I had another two years' worth of sales to start sifting through for my third *100 Best* book.

I didn't actually start writing *Ka-Ching* until late February, and I really put the pressure on myself, my brother Lee, my printer Becky, and my editor Susan. We had a target publishing date of July 7, 2007. 777. I thought that would be really cool! We made it with a galley edition, but just by the skin of our teeth. Lee, Becky, and Susan are awesome to work with and I want to say a big thank you to them!!!

That book contained stories about a lot of kooky things that would have been easy to overlook at garage and estate sales. It didn't have the stories about huge dollar sales that *Money Making Madness* did (which includes descriptions of two items that sold for over $2,000). My most expensive single item in *Ka-Ching* was $1,150.

The big hits were becoming fewer and farther apart. But that is consistent with what I have always taught: you make your money selling $18 items (my average sales price) day in and day out. If you sit around and wait for the home runs (the title of this book!) instead of taking the base hits, you won't be able to pay your bills.

Now, let's learn a little bit more about the fourth book in this series. I am so proud and happy to announce *The 4th 100 Best Things I've Sold on eBay: Home Run*

Home Run....The 4th 100 Best Things I've Sold on eBay

Every time I write a new book in this series, it is hard to come up with a catch phrase to make it memorable. My mom had a great idea (which she does on many occasions). She suggested I have a name-the-book contest for my 15,000 ezine readers (receive my free ezine by signing up at www.TheQueenofAuctions.com).

One of my ezine readers wrote in with the wonderful title, "Home Run." I love it for a couple of reasons. First, there are four bases and now there are four books. Second, my son and daughter are serious baseball contenders, and I love the all-American pastime.

Unfortunately, we couldn't identify the name of the ezine subscriber who sent in the winning title before press time. I searched my emails without success, and Mo's computer had crashed so she couldn't help. I want and need to give credit where credit is deserved, but it was not meant to be. We will figure it out and take care of it as soon as we can.

One fact that's obvious in this book: eBay has evolved since we start-ed our business, and so have we. I now sell about 50% of my $10,000 monthly sales out of my eBay store. If you don't have an eBay store yet, you must set one up. It is not difficult to do, and it doubles your selling opportunities. eBay stores are just a different, yet simple, alternative to selling at auction. Once you have listed something at auction and it doesn't sell, you can move it into your eBay "store" at a fixed price for as little as three cents a month (for items up to $24.99). The work of writing up the item has already been done, so there is no down side to listing it in a store.

Thank you so much for buying this book. I hope you enjoy reading it as much as I enjoyed writing it. Happy eBaying!

Lynn

eBay® Home Run

#1 Antique Turquoise Brooch

$0.⁰⁰ Paid

From: Inheritance

Antique Turquoise Bar Pin Brooch L. Reid London in Box!

Description:
This is an amazing 1880s or so piece. It is 2" long and the center portion is about ½" round. Gold-filled yellow with tiny turquoise stones. Needs a little repair around the edge. The box says, "Art Jewellers L. Reid Established 1843 62 Strand London WC." An awesome piece of antiquity. My brother who is a GIA certified gemologist has checked this piece for me.

Winning Bid:

$54.⁵⁰

Ended: 7/25/06
History: 2 bids
Starting Bid: $49.99
Winner: Massachusetts

Viewed
 X

Antique Turquoise Brooch #1

The Story

It was summer and very hot in Palm Desert—no kidding! We were waiting for baseball to be finished for the year so that we could go up to Bellingham for a month. Can you believe that we play baseball year-round except for the month of August? Crazy! The boys start in September and finish the end of July. It really is a serious commitment.

Talking about serious commitments, that was how my grandmother always viewed her antiques business. It wasn't a hobby, it wasn't a way to pass time—it was a business that always made her money. Don't get me wrong—it was also her passion, and she would rather be working than doing practically anything else (I am very lucky to be like her in that respect). But she was always thinking about ways to make her business more profitable.

Back in the 1960s, she had the amazing idea to start bringing containers of antiques back from Europe. She was way before her time, and I think it was because of all those hours she spent thinking. My grandmother's niece, Gwen Sussex, told me the other day that her father Houston (my Grandma's brother) would often sit, tapping his fingers on a table while looking into space. She would ask him, "Daddy, what are you doing?" and he would answer, "Thinking."

I was like "Wow—I have goose bumps!" My grandma did the same thing. It was probably during one of those thinking episodes that she came up with the container idea as a way to make sure she could legally write off her travel expenses. I don't know what my grandma loved more: traveling, her antiques business, jewelry, or her three grandchildren.

But I do know this: if my grandmother could combine traveling with business, that would be a win-win situation. One of her favorite places to shop was Portobello Road in London. I am guessing that she bought this turquoise brooch there about 1960 and had it shipped home in a container.

When I didn't see any garage sales in Palm Desert that hot day in July, I started going through some of the boxes that I inherited from my G (that was one of our terms of endearment for my grandmother). I found this brooch, and it was marked "$125 GF (Gold Filled) Turquoise."

That meant that my brother Lee had checked it out and had determined it wasn't gold. I thought it was beautiful and decided to list it at a starting price of $49.99. What was really neat about this piece was that it came in the original box from the jeweler. By the way, these antique jewelry boxes (even empty) can sell for serious money.

The brooch didn't sell for much more than $49.99, but I was happy and knew that my grandmother had probably only paid a few quid for it back in the 1960s. When other people were experimenting with drugs, my grandmother was experimenting with business.

#2 Native American Hatpin

$0.⁰⁰ Paid

From: Inheritance

Hatpin Hat Pin Native American Indian Jamestown 1907!

Description:

This is an amazing and rare piece. 8" long and 1¾" wide. The top has a Native American chief or woman? and says "Jamestown 1807 to 1907." Must be some type of anniversary piece. In great condition. Needs polishing. Don't know if it is sterling because I couldn't find any maker's marks.

Winning Bid:

$62.⁰²

Ended: 7/25/06
History: 13 bids
Starting Bid: $9.99
Winner: Texas

Viewed

000083 X

Native American Hatpin #2

The Story

I knew this was a good piece when I immediately started receiving questions about it. The first question was, "Could you add a photo to your auction page that shows a close-up of the back, especially a profile view of the finding (small piece that holds the top onto the pin)?"

I answered back, "Hi, unfortunately I am out of town and can't take a photo. If I remember correctly, it looked original to me. I have seen hatpins put together from buttons and other items but this one appears original."

Of course, I had seen hatpins made from many other items because, yes, you guessed it, Cheryl Leaf loved to make hatpins. She would find antique buttons, round pieces of jewelry and brooches and solder hat pin stems on them. She knew that hatpin collectors were a serious bunch and she decided she could help them out and make herself some money—well, why not?

But let's figure out what a hatpin is before we go any further. Hatpins are used (typically in pairs) to hold a hat onto the head by using a woman's hair. The most decorative part is the pinhead. My hatpin head was really neat. Hatpins were originally invented to hold wimples and veils in place and were handmade in Britain.

So what's a wimple? Wimples were head coverings worn by women in medieval Europe; they were worn around the neck and chin. Wimples were developed as a way to honor the bible verse that states that an unmarried woman should not show her hair. Yikes!

But back to the hatpins like the one I sold. In 1832, an American machine was invented to produce hatpins, which made them much more affordable for the masses.

What made my hatpin so collectible was its design and the fact that it was an original hatpin—not handmade by Cheryl Leaf! Jamestown was the first permanent English settlement in North America (located in Virginia) and was named after King James I of England. Jamestown was founded on May 14, 1607. As I write this story, I realize that my hatpin must have said "1607 1907" (rather than the "1807 1907" I had used in my description).

You see, Jamestown hosted a type of World's Fair in 1907, and the official symbol was that of a Native American chief shaking the hand of an Englishman. My hatpin was just the Indian chief, but was obviously still very collectible. I got over $62 for it and I am sure that my grandmother didn't pay more than $1 for it.

Pretty cool! I think I will go and find Indiana and put a wimple on her to show you what they looked like. Indy is going to kill me for this one!

#3 Hawaiian Charm Bracelet

$0.⁰⁰ Paid

From: Inheritance

Sterling Vintage Eames Hawaii Hawaiiana Charm Bracelet

Description:

This is an amazing bracelet. Almost all of the charms are marked "Sterling." There are 7 charms, one for each of the Hawaiian Islands. 8" long. I would guess 1940s to 1960s Eames era. Needs polishing. Hawaii, Nihau, Kauai, Oahu, Molokai, Lanai and Maui. This is an awesome piece that won't last long. Don't let it pass you by!

Winning Bid:

$32.⁹⁸

Ended: 7/25/06
History: 2 bids
Starting Bid: $9.99
Winner: Carmel, CA

Viewed

000104 X

Hawaiian Charm Bracelet #3

The Story

The first time I went to Hawaii was in 1988 with my friend Anna Maria Hurtado Erbabian Zipperhead Junior the 3rd. O.K., that isn't really her name, but somehow it ended up being her nickname. Her "official" name is Annie Hurtado and she is one of my best friends from college.

I hadn't talked to Annie for a while and about five days ago, someone called my eBay office line and Indiana picked it up. Indy yelled to me, "There is someone with a baby zipper head on the phone for you." I thought, "What?" and decided I had better take the call—it sounded scary. I said, "Hello?" and heard, "Hi, Lynn Adelle." Then I knew who it was— Annie—and realized she had used her full ridiculous nickname.

Scared the daylights out of Indy. But it was great to catch up with Annie. We talked a little bit about the crazy trip to Maui that we couldn't afford when we took it in 1988. My motto was always, "Charge your youth on credit cards and travel as much as you can. You have the rest of your life to repay the money—but you won't get your youth back."

I fell in love with Hawaii on that first trip. I spent my thirtieth birthday in Hawaii, my fortieth birthday in Spain, and I really wonder where I am going to spend my fiftieth. Well, I have plenty of time to figure that out.

But back to Hawaii. As you know, my grandma loved to travel. Hawaii and Australia were on her "to do" list, so she took (almost) everyone to Honolulu, Hawaii for a family trip in 1983. I didn't get to go because I was in classes at college. Bummer! It took me until 1988 to finally make it to the Aloha State.

Hawaii wasn't really my grandmother's type of vacation. She didn't like the sun. And apparently, neither did my sister after that trip. It turns out that my family (without my guidance) left Kiki and my brother Lee at an outdoor water park all day long with NO sunscreen. My sister developed huge sunburn blisters on her back.

Even though my grandma didn't like the sun, she loved any new opportunity to shop for her store. I think we still have many touristy things that she bought on that trip that we are all trying to sell on eBay. This bracelet that I sold for $33 might have been one of those items!

Vintage Hawaiiana (like the bracelet) is awesome and will always sell, but most of the touristy things my grandmother bought in the 1980s (such as pineapple key rings and bottle openers) have not done so well. I'm hoping that those are getting more collectible with every passing day.

My grandmother never fulfilled her dream of visiting Australia. That was something she regretted to the very end. My grandmother would have agreed with the idea I included in my auction description—don't let the things you want pass you by! Take advantage of the opportunities you have today, because you never know how many tomorrows you will have.

#4 Dansk Cherry Dinnerware

$45.00/17
Paid
From: eBay

Dansk Bing Cherry Cherries Red Bands 2 Dinner Plates NICE

Description:
2 Dinner Plates. 11". This is a great pattern. Dansk Bing Cherry only made from 2003 to 2004—it is now discontinued. Red rings/bands/stripes with red cherries cherry center. Hand painted, made in China. We have a lot of pieces in this wonderful pattern up for sale this week. All in great condition. No chips, no cracks, no crazing.

Winning Bid: **$126.45/9**

Ended: 7/30/06
History: 20 bids/9 auctions
Starting Bid: $9.99 ea
Winner: NJ, MI

Viewed
000162 X

Dansk Cherry Dinnerware #4

The Story

Finally, a story about something I bought myself! And to make it even more interesting, I bought it on eBay. It was July of 2006 and I was getting ready to teach my first Live Boot Camp. I was extremely nervous about it.

I wanted it to be the best experience EVER for my first nine students. I had been working on the event with my mentor, Kevin Nations. The event had been looming in my future like a monster, and I was terrified to think about it. Kevin was going to be in Florida at Mark Victor Hansen's *Mega Book Marketing* seminar, and Peter and I were also going to attend.

In Orlando at the seminar, Kevin and I sat down and hammered out the schedule. He assured me that my first Live Boot Camp was going to be an incredible success. Kevin also told me that my nine students (Lynette, Janet, Saul, Linda, Jen, Pat, Louise, Lia, and CJ) would take away life-long lessons and invaluable experiences.

I thanked him for the vote of confidence, and off Peter and I went to swim with the manatees in a Florida River. It was so scary, but I plugged my nose and jumped in with the huge mammals (and a crocodile). Yikes! The manatees turned out to be as sweet as you can imagine and the croc kept its distance.

As soon as I flew back to Palm Desert, I decided that to make my first boot camp even better, I would buy a set of dishes on eBay and demonstrate how to sell them back on eBay for profit. I bought this Dansk set on eBay (seventeen pieces) for $33 plus $12 shipping, so I was in for $45.

I sold the dinner plates for $11 each at auction! I sold some of the other pieces for their starting bid of $9.99. All told, I received $126.45 in nine auctions for items I paid $45 for on eBay. I proved that you didn't have to leave your house to make money selling on the Internet!

The key to this success story was using the Dralle Method and also being able to identify the pattern. The eBay seller from whom I bought this set had NOT put the pattern name in her title. Her mistake was my good fortune.

My first boot camp took place the last week in July at the Lodge in Rancho Mirage. The first student to enter the room was Saul. After the weekend was over he told me this: "My wife signed up to attend, but I told her she was crazy. I didn't believe in you or any of this. I told Anne that I would take her place to prove my point. An hour into the class I called Anne and told her, 'This girl is the real deal.'" That made all my hard work worthwhile!

The key to making my first Live Boot Camp such a success was careful planning, being passionate about helping others, not being afraid of the monsters and plugging my nose and jumping in! I hope you always plug your nose and just jump in.

#5 Johnny Depp Disney Pin

$8.⁹⁵ Paid

From: World of Disney, WDW

Walt Disney World Pirates Caribbean New Pin Johnny Depp

Description:

Johnny Depp pin is brand-new on card. 1½" by ½". Captain Jack Sparrow's face. We have a lot of Walt Disney World Pirates of the Caribbean Curse of the Black Pearl up for sale. I just got back from Orlando and they are all in excellent brand new condition.

Winning Bid:

$13.⁴⁹

Ended: 7/30/0
History: 2 bids
Starting Bid: $9.99
Winner: Indiana

Viewed
 X

Johnny Depp Disney Pin #5

The Story

Speaking of mistakes made by sellers, I am not one to talk. I make mistakes all the time! You will be reading about my biggest mistake ever later in this book (story #36). But in this story, I was still in Florida and Peter and I decided to go out for a nice dinner in Downtown Disney. We chose Fulton's Crab House, which is a floating steamboat that has amazing shellfish. We love crab and lobster!

After dinner we walked around and were fascinated by all the pin trading that was going on. I had never heard of such a thing! A light bulb went off in my head—I could buy a bunch (and I do mean a bunch) of these pins and sell them for big bucks on eBay!

Well, if you know me, you know I am fast and I make decisions quickly. Before you could say "Supercalifragilisticexpialidocious" (we were at Disney World) I had purchased about $500 worth of trading pins.

The pins, about 50 of them, ranged

in retail price from $8.95 to $19.95. I thought they were going to sell for big bucks on eBay. Wrong again. I got back to Palm Desert and got them all listed at auction the end of July. Out of my 50 pins, only one sold. It had a picture of Johnny Depp on it and I think it sold because Pirates of the Caribbean had just come out.

I had paid $8.95 for the trading pin and it sold on eBay for $13.49. I had made $4.54 on my $500 purchase. Not so great.

I did learn a valuable lesson: stop, look, listen, research, and think before you spend $500 on anything. If I had done my research, I might have learned that the trading pins with a hidden Mickey Mouse can be more valuable. The pins with Mickey are only given to cast members, and you have to actually trade with the cast members who work at the stores to get them. For those of you who have attended an eBay Live, you know how crazy the pin-trading frenzy can get!

So, to make pin trading profitable, what you want to do is buy a bunch of cheap trading pins from the traders who have set up shop all over Downtown Disney. Once you have your cheap pins, you go looking for the cast members who are wearing lanyards. (A lanyard is a cord that is worn around the neck to hold something).

When you spot a pin on a cast member's lanyard that has the hidden Mickey Mouse, you trade them one of your cheap pins for it. But don't spend too much—lots of these hidden Mickey pins only sell for around $1.

The good news is this: one and a half years after I purchased the pins, I only have thirteen left in my eBay store. They have been selling, slowly but surely.

Lesson learned. And now I just don't know what to say, so I will end with "Supercalifragilisticexpialidocious."

And according to the 1964 Walt Disney film *Mary Poppins*, that superlong word is defined as "What you say when you don't know what to say."

#6 Vintage Halliburton Case

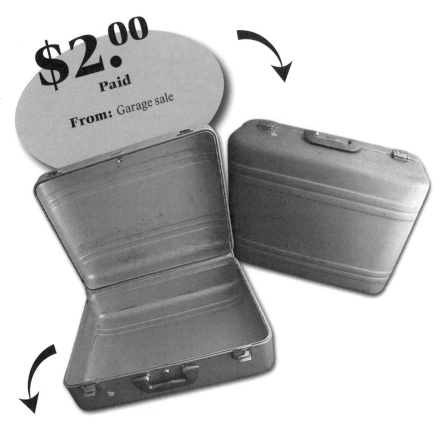

$2.00
Paid
From: Garage sale

Zero Centurion Elite Halliburton Vintage Hard Suitcase

Description:

Zero Centurion Elite Halliburton Vintage Hard Suitcase. Says "2392" on the key hole. No key. Aluminum or silver-colored metal and I would guess Eames era 1960s to 1970s. It is about 21" by 7.5" by 17". Needs a good cleaning. There are nicks and dings on this piece. Still a very neat item to protect your valuables when traveling.

Winning Bid:

$57.00

Ended: 8/12/06
History: 13 bids
Starting Bid: $9.99
Winner: Los Angeles, CA

Viewed

000277 X

Vintage Halliburton Case   #6

The Story

It was still the summer of 2006 and my kids had been out of the desert since July 15th. They attended a family reunion with their dad in Oregon and then their grandpa drove down to pick them up and drive them to Bellingham. I didn't see them for four weeks, and that is why I was able to travel so much on my own that summer.

It can get pretty lonely in my big house with no kids, so I was very busy listing on eBay and doing some traveling. One of the weeks I was home, I decided to walk around and find huge items that I could sell to free up some space. In a corner was this neat suitcase that I had bought at a garage sale for $2. It had been my intention to use it to decorate my house, but I had never gotten around to making that happen. That August, it got my attention because several weeks before, I had seen a similar one at a professionally run estate sale, and the lady wanted $25 for it.

I thought, "Hmmm, this may be a good piece." I decided I could use $9.99 more than I could use a dusty aluminum suitcase I had never used. Well, guess what. The company that made it, Zero Halliburton, turned out to be incredibly interesting.

The company began in 1938 when Earle P. Halliburton, a globetrotting businessman (was that even possible back then?) hired a team of aircraft engineers to design an aluminum suit case that could endure his constant and rough traveling. Earle used to travel through the Texas oil fields in the back of a pick up truck, which was very hard on his luggage. The new aluminum case was hard-wearing,

weather resistant, and every case was strong enough to stand on.

These cases became known as Halliburton cases. In 1952, Mr. Halliburton sold his travel case division to the Zero Corporation (a metal fabrication company formerly known as Zierold). The new division of the Zero Co. was then known as Zero Halliburton.

These cases have appeared in over 200 movies and television shows. And most notably, the Nuclear Football (the briefcase used by the US President to order a nuclear attack) is a modified Zero Halliburton case.

Pretty cool! So my case was definitely made after 1952 and ended up selling for $57. Awesome! New, these cases can sell for $200 to $700—so no wonder my used one did so well. What I found most fascinating was that it was shipped to San Vicente Boulevard in Brentwood, California (an area of LA) to zip code 90049.

That was where I lived for seven years after college. It brought back great memories: Mom's Saloon, Westward Ho Market, The Duck Blind, Chin Chins, La Scala Presto, All American Burger, and Flair Cleaners. I miss those Brentwood days just like I missed my kids those four weeks that summer. Oh well—$55 profit always makes me feel better.

#7 Dansk Thistle Flatware

$25.00 Paid

From: Thrift Store, Sedona, AZ

DANSK $25—

IMQ Dansk France Thistle 1 Stainless Dinner Fork HTF

Description:

Hard to find. 7½" 3-tine. We have a lot of pieces of this stainless steel pattern up for sale this week in separate auctions. All are signed with "Dansk France" and "IMQ," which means that it was designed by Jens Quistgaard—one of the founders of Dansk and their premier designer. All pieces are in very good to excellent condition. Slight wear as can be expected. This pattern was made from 1969 to 1996 and is currently discontinued. The pattern name is Thistle. Very hard to find.

Winning Bid: $468.58/49

Ended: 8/19/06
History: 169 bids/49 auctions
Starting Bid: $3.99 - $9.99
Winner: IL, AK, NE, AZ, NC, Can, UK

Viewed

001093 X

Dansk Thistle Flatware #7

The Story

Since my kids were in good hands, it was time to do some more traveling *sin niños*. I met Peter in Sedona, AZ the first week in August. We chose Sedona because it was a 5 1/2 hour drive for each of us. We were going to be staying at the Enchantment Resort, which was offering really great rates because it was summer.

I got to town early, so on my way to the resort, I stopped off at a cute little local thrift store. Talk about a score! I found a set of Dansk flatware for $25 and two cat paintings. You will hear more about those cat paintings in the next story.

The Dansk was made in France (which you rarely see!). Most of the Dansk flatware I run across is made in Japan and Korea. I knew this was going to be a great find and hopefully pay for the trip.

Sedona was awesome and beautiful (especially the red rocks), but there wasn't much night life. By the time we would get into town at 9 pm for dinner, everything was closed! Oh well—it was a really great vacation anyway.

As soon as I got back to Palm Desert, I immediately listed the Dansk flatware. I had 49 pieces and I listed them all individually at $9.99 each. About half of the set sold the first time at auction. The most expensive piece that sold was a single dinner fork for $17.50!

This was in the old days when I used to list twice at auction, the first time with a starting price of $9.99 and (if it didn't sell) a second auction starting at $3.99. All the rest of the set sold the second time at auction.

If I had those pieces today, I would have let them sit in my eBay store at a higher price and wait for the right buyer, instead of giving them away for $3.99 at auction.

The buyers of the Dansk lived everywhere from Alaska to Nebraska, Canada and even the UK! What a popular pattern. Most of the buyers had chosen this pattern for their everyday stainless when they got married. Some buyers were still married and some were divorced and yet still using the flatware!

Here is an email from one of the still-married buyers: "In 1978 I married and moved to London. This pattern was my selection for daily flatware on my bridal list. I have used it ever since and over the years pieces have been lost, for some reason a lot of spoons! I regret that Dansk discontinued the pattern as I believe it to be classic and timeless. Judging by the amount of interest in bidders on eBay, they should reissue it!" (Sara, London).

Don't you just love selling flatware and china patterns on eBay? Not only do we make money (a lot of it) but we are helping people find things they need. eBay is such a cool place! Just like Sedona.

#8 Pischner Siamese Watercolor

$5.⁰⁰

Paid

From: Thrift Store, Sedona, AZ

G Grace Pischner Miller Siamese Cat Watercolor Eames

Description:

An original watercolor by Grace Pischner, 1912 to 1991. She was
born in Washington State on January 12, 1912 and worked primarily in watercolors. She specialized in seascapes of California. The
cat looks to be Eames era 1950s or 1960s. Not what she typically
painted. 18" by 7½". In a 1960s wooden frame. There is a tiny tear
at the top that I have shown in a photo. Pischner exhibited widely in
the San Diego, CA area. She was among the founding members of
the San Diego Painting Society and was also a long-time member
of the La Jolla Art Association. She died in San Diego on April 12,
1991. Her works typically sell for hundreds of dollars.

Winning Bid:

$99.⁰⁰

Ended: 8/29/06
History: 1 bid
Starting Bid: $99.00
Winner: Kansas

Viewed

 X

Pischner Siamese Watercolor #8

The Story

In that same Sedona thrift store, I found a very interesting mid-century modern oil painting of a cat on wood as well as a watercolor of a Siamese cat. The oil was $3 and the watercolor $5. I think I probably paid more for the watercolor because it was framed.

I couldn't make out the signature on the oil painting but I could read the G. Pischner signature on the Siamese watercolor (Don't you just love it when you can actually READ a signature?)!

When I got back to Palm Desert, I immediately Googled G. Pischner and found that the "G." stood for Grace. She was a pretty famous painter and was originally from Washington State. Just like me! Grace relocated to Southern California (San Diego). Also just like me! She specialized in seascapes (not like me!) so this painting was outside her norm. I found that Grace's paintings ranged from $139 to $275 on an artist gallery website. I decided to list both of my paintings at a starting bid of $99. There may not be a lot of demand for the two paintings, so I was prepared to wait for the right buyer.

Well, much to my surprise and happiness, the Pischner painting sold for $99. The mod oil did not sell. So, I wrote on the *I Sell* sheet to list it at $99 in my eBay store. Unfortunately, it got relisted at $9.99 and darn it—sold within two hours of being relisted!

I hate it when that happens. Oh well, I got $110 for an $8 investment for the two paintings, plus $468 on a $25 flatware investment while on vacation! How often in this world can you turn $33 into $578 in seven days?

And I got to learn about a very talented Washington artist. My great grandmother, Maybelle, was an artist and I have the only two paintings of hers that remain. One was painted in 1898. I remember the day my grandmother called me to tell me that she had uncovered a huge painting of Maybelle's in the attic and asked if I would like it. "Of course!" I said. My grandma wrapped it with great care and asked my friend Brad Wiesner's father to hand-carry it from Bellingham to me in Southern California. What a precious piece.

I love to know that I have two personal pieces from Maybelle's short life. She was my grandma Cheryl Leaf's mother, and she gave birth to Cheryl in 1912—the same year that Grace was born. Luckily, I got to see my grandmother live until the year 2000. Grace Pischner lived until 1991. Maybelle only lived until she was 30 and died in 1913 when my grandmother was only eighteen months old. Don't forget how precious life is and be thankful for God's grace.

#9 Montgolfiere Dinner Set

$60.^{00}
Paid
From: Thrift Store Palm Desert

Williams Sonoma Montgolfiere Plate Green Hot Air Balloon

Description:

One 7½" salad plate. Hot air balloon in green with banners or flags flying from the basket. The pattern is "Montgolfiere" by Williams Sonoma. Blue and white cloud background. The salad plates are all different vintage hot air balloons. The soup bowl just has the clouds. A really neat and expensive pattern. Made in Japan and decorated in the U.S. These pieces are in perfect condition.

Winning Bid:

$480.^{75}/36

Ended: 8/29/06
History: 74 bids/36 auctions
Starting Bid: $9.99 ea auction
Winner: AZ, CA, NJ

Viewed

000942 X

Montgolfiere Dinner Set #9

The Story

I was back in Palm Desert with just a week to go before I would fly home to Bellingham for two weeks. It was going to be a crazy two weeks. We were planning to celebrate my mom's 70th birthday, I would be doing an autographing session at Village Books in Fairhaven, I was trying to find a tenant for my rental house, and on top of all that I was going to do a Live Boot Camp in Bellingham. Was I crazy? Yes, and for those of you who know me—I still am! I always take on huge projects...it is what makes life interesting.

In that one week here in the desert, I knew I had to find some high quality, easy-to-list items. I had been watching this set of china at my local thrift store for some time. They had probably done some research on it because they wanted $15 per salad plate, $5 per soup bowl, and $5 per mug. Yikes. I waited until it was marked down to $5 per plate and $2.50 each for the soup bowls and mugs and then I waited some more until it went half price. Patience is a virtue. I paid $60 for 36 pieces.

I got these listed and ready to sell so that the auctions would end while I was in Bellingham. Williams Sonoma is a very good brand name. The company opened its first store in 1956 and carried fine quality French cookware. Since then it has opened 250 stores across the United States. Today, its stores carry a wide range of high-quality items for the home. The dinnerware set I had purchased had been designed specifically for Williams Sonoma. The

salad plates in this pattern listed for $33.99 each on Replacements.com and the dinner plates listed for $75.99 each! Too bad I didn't have any of those dinner plates.

Now where in the world did they come up with the name for this pattern? It turns out that "Montgolfiere" is the name for a standard hot air balloon, because the hot air balloon was invented by the Montgolfier brothers in 1783 in France. Pretty interesting!

We have a lot of hot air balloons here in the desert, and when my dad was visiting during his 70th birthday in 2004, I suggested that he might like to ride in one for his special day. My dad is very conservative and he didn't want me to spend so much money on him, so he passed.

So while these hot air balloon plates, bowls and mugs were selling, I was in Bellingham celebrating my mom's 70th birthday. Now, she didn't go up in a hot air balloon either, but the $420 profit I made on these dishes helped to pay for her 70th birthday at the beach. We had a 1950s themed party and everyone wore costumes. Is that what the Williams and Sonoma staff looked like when they opened their first store in 1956? I certainly hope not!

#10 Nambe Covered Pan

$9.00 Paid

From: Garage sale, Bellingham, WA

Nambe 2 Piece Casserole 13 Covered Aluminum Modern NICE

Description:
Covered casserole is signed "Nambe 13" and measures 6.5" by 10.25". In good condition with the usual wear. Needs cleaning. Not rounded, but more rectangular and squarish.

Winning Bid: **$51.00**

Ended: 9/1/06
History: 18 bids
Starting Bid: $9.99
Winner: WV

Viewed

000128 X

Nambe Covered Pan #10

The Story

It is always fun to stay at my mom's beach house for a few weeks every summer. It gets us out of the hot desert sun and next to the ocean. I love the ocean, and hope to live near it someday (at least part-time)!

The garage sales in Bellingham during the summer are always amazing. It turned out that I was there for the annual Sandy Point community garage sale. Sandy Point is on a spit on the open ocean. It is not sheltered, and during the winter can be pretty scary with huge waves and flooding—but during the summer it is beautiful.

The community garage sale brings out a crowd. We always run into people we know and it is a lot of fun. There are hot dog stands, kids selling lemonade, and it is like a big party as we rush from sale to sale.

I always buy way more than I should and then have to figure out what should get shipped back to California and what to leave. It is such an adrenaline rush that I just can't help myself.

At one sale, I turned over a covered casserole dish and was excited to see it was marked "Nambe." It was priced at $15. Yikes! Quite a bit for a garage sale. I told the seller I loved the dish but that $15 was more than I could spend. She suggested $9 and I had a heavy pan to take home to California. Will I ever learn? Probably not.

The reason I wanted this pan so badly was because Nambe always sells. Nambe was established in New Mexico in 1953 by Pauline Platt Cable. She and her husband Peter partnered with a metallurgist, who designed an eight-metal alloy that retains both hot and cold temperatures for long periods of time. The alloy resembles silver, can be used for both oven baking and stovetop cooking, and never needs polishing. What a cool metal! I was very wrong in calling it aluminum in my title. Ooops!

The company "Nambe Ware" was born, named for an ancient village not far from Santa Fe, whose name means, "Born of the earth and the fertile imagination." Each item is cast in individually prepared molds made from black sand. Nambe is still going strong today and is recognized worldwide for its award-winning designs and admired for its dedication to artistic integrity and everyday functionality.

The factory was originally located in Pojoaque, New Mexico, on Highway 85; after three factory fires, however, it was relocated to Silver Road in Santa Fe. Nambe's website says that, "If your timing is right, you may find select seconds and overstocks at prices up to 65% off." Sounds like a plan to me!

I was very happy that my Nambe pan sold for $51. I thought it was neat that while I was enjoying the beautiful oceanside environment in Bellingham, I found the Nambe pan that was born of the earth and fertile imagination of the desert.

#11 Cranberry Lamp Shade

$1.⁰⁰ Paid

From: Senior Center sale, Bellingham, WA

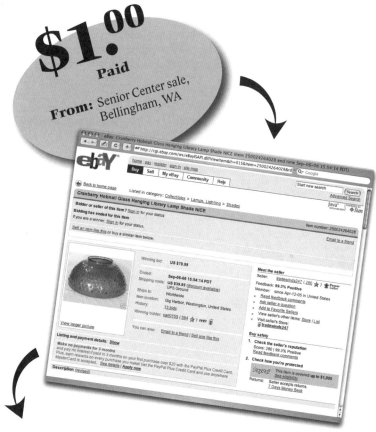

Cranberry Hobnail Glass Hanging Library Lamp Shade NICE

Description:

Beautiful vintage cranberry hanging library, parlor lamp shade is 14" at the base or fitter and is 8" tall. Hobnail bump design. No chips no cracks no crazing. In excellent condition. Might be a Fenton shade but it is not signed.

Winning Bid:

$79.⁹⁹

Ended: 9/6/06
History: 13 bids
Starting Bid: $9.99
Winner: Texas

Viewed

000082 X

Cranberry Lamp Shade #11

The Story

My first Live Boot Camp in Palm Springs in July of 2006 had been such a home run and so fun that I decided to take my dog and pony show on the road and host one in Bellingham. I had no idea what I was getting myself into. Or did I? And just what is a dog and pony show?

"Dog and pony show" was a term used in the late-19th century to refer to small traveling circuses that toured through small towns and rural areas; they featured performances by dogs and ponies as the main attractions. I guess I was going to be the main attraction at my event!

To illustrate just what a huge traveling show Boot Camp was, I ended up shipping at least twelve boxes of things to Bellingham for the three-day event. Then I went out shopping in Bellingham to make sure I had at least 100 items to write up and list in front of my students. I was certainly out of my mind, because I knew I would eventually have to ship this all back to California.

My mom, brother and sister were all on hand to help. We had a smaller group, just five students: Michelle, Cat, Sharla, Anne and Saul. It turned out to be an awesome experience.

Saul had already attended the first Live Boot Camp, and this time he brought his wife, Anne. Saul was our comic relief. As we were driving to garage sales on Saturday, I was bragging that I never get lost in my home town.

As soon as I said it, we ended up leaving half our group at a garage sale in Edgmoor. Didn't even notice that we had lost them, and Edgmoor is the area of town where I grew up! Boy, did I have egg on my face.

Speaking of eggs, we ended up at a rummage sale (I love the word "rummage") at the senior center. The sale was awesome and (this is where the egg comes in) they actually had a kitchen open and were serving egg-salad sandwiches for $2. I love egg salad, so I got in line to order one. The lady serving asked me, "Did you go to Sehome High School?" I said (quite tentatively), "Yes." And she said "I worked in the cafeteria and I remember you." You have got to love growing up in a small town!

At that sale, Sharla from Denver found this incredible cranberry lamp shade for $1. I encouraged her to buy it even though she had already bought a lot of huge items (bikes, furniture, and so on), and we hadn't figured out how to get them back to Denver for her.

She listed the shade during the Live Boot Camp, and it got thirteen bids and sold for $79.99! Saul and Anne were such sweethearts that they drove this precious shade home to Gig Harbor and actually shipped it to the winner for Sharla.

My Live Boot Camps are like a fun circus—even if I do sometimes end up with egg on my face!

#12 Yankee Candle Tarts

Yankee Candle 7 Wax Tarts Aroma MIP Patchouli Clove

Description:

7 wax tarts from the Yankee Candle Company still mint in the original plastic. We carried these in our antiques and gift store so came directly from the factory. They have been carefully stored for a few years. Brownish orange color and the scent is Patchouli and Clove from the Aroma line. Discontinued.

Winning Bid: **$208.⁰⁶/4**

Ended: 9/6/06
History: 49 bids/4
Starting Bid: $9.99 ea auction
Winner: CA, VA, PA

Viewed
000129 X

Yankee Candle Tarts #12

The Story

My sister, Kiki, had her son Zach in April of 2006 and she wanted to be a stay-at-home mom. It was hard for her to list on eBay because the baby was still very small and he took up a lot of her time, so she decided to have a garage sale with stuff she inherited from our grandmother. Despite her decision, she never got around to actually holding the garage sale (thank goodness)!

Among the things that she had priced for her sale was a basket full of Yankee Candle tarts. These are candles shaped like miniature pies; they are designed to be burned in a tart warmer. They were originally 95 cents each in our store, and Kiki had marked them ten cents each for her garage sale.

At the same time that this was going on, we were getting ready for my mom's big seventieth birthday party. My mom needed candles, so my sister brought the tarts over. I looked at them and said, "You know—tarts do not have wicks. Good luck burning those!" We all laughed and my sister took the basket back to her house.

Fast forward a week to the day before I was set to return to California. I told my sister that I would stop by her house to list 50 things from her garage sale pile for her.

I randomly grabbed items. I took all 29 of the Yankee tarts, some Eddie Walker Christmas ornaments, a handful of beads, and some collectibles. I decided to sell the tarts in groupings of five, seven, seven, and ten, matched according to scent. As I was writing them up, I thought to myself—what am I doing? These are never going to sell! They were only 95 cents originally in the shop, and they never sold there. We all inherited handfuls of them. But I decided to go with the flow and trust my original instinct.

Well, guess what? Of the 50 items I listed for my sister, eighteen sold at auction. Within the next two weeks, four more items sold from her eBay store for a total of 22 sales. She still has the other 28 items listed in her eBay store and I believe that a high percentage of those will eventually sell. Grand total—$425.99! From a garage sale pile that she would have been lucky to get $100 for (plus all the aggravation). This is proof!!! Never have a garage sale!!

And the icing on the cake—or should I say on the tart? The auction with seven bergamot and mandarin Yankee Candle tarts (marketed as the "Balancing" fragrance) sold for $23.06, the auction with five sage and citrus ("Relaxing") sold for $53.55, the auction with ten mixed candle tarts (two "Passionate," three "Cleansing" and five "Stimulating") for $57.89 and the auction with seven patchouli and clove ("Rejuvenating") tarts sold for (drum roll, please) ...$73.56!! There is a huge following for retired Yankee Candle tarts, and that was what these were. Who knew?

I will tell you this. I have been out digging through the boxes I inherited from the shop sniffing for my Yankee tarts. I just hope they haven't melted!

#13 Swedish Door Chime

25¢
Paid
From: Garage sale, Bellingham, WA

Swedish Door Chimes Valkommen Sweden Rosemaling NEAT

Description:
Neat Swedish door chime. 7½" by 8⅜". In good condition. Needs cleaning. One ball is missing. Vintage Eames era 1950s to 1970s. Darling. "Valkommen" means "welcome" in Swedish.

Winning Bid:

$14.¹⁵

Ended: 9/12/06
History: 3
Starting Bid: $9.99
Winner: Aichi, Japan

Viewed
000024 X

Swedish Door Chime   #13

The Story

This was one of the many items I had purchased in Bellingham to demonstrate the Dralle Method at my Live Boot Camp. I paid 25 cents for it at a garage sale and my mom had done the write-up on my *I Sell* sheet during the event. I didn't get it listed until I got back to California.

The beauty of the Dralle Method is that you can list from anywhere! So, while this item was being shipped back to Palm Desert from my Bellingham dog and pony show, I got it listed. This piece spoke to me because it said "Welcome" in Swedish, and my grandmother Cheryl Leaf was half Swedish; my grandfather Elmer Leaf was 100% Swedish.

I think "welcome" is a great word to describe my grandmother. She welcomed her customers into her antique store with a warm smile, she welcomed friends and family into her home with an, "Are you hungry? What can I make you to eat?" She loved to have company.

After I listed the door chime on eBay, I got a phone call from my dad saying that my stepmom Sue's *Good Housekeeping* had arrived in the mail, and I was featured in an article! Can you believe it? I had been working with a writer at GH since January of 2006. Patricia Greco was awesome and worked tirelessly to get me in the magazine.

Finally, there was a place for me in a new column called "Money." The article was entitled, "Dream Job: How She built an eBay Antiques Empire."

It appeared in the September 2006 issue. I ran to my local Ralph's Grocery store and bought 30 copies.

It was such an adrenaline rush when the checker I've known for four years asked, "Why are you buying so many?" and I could actually answer, "I am on page 62!"

My grandmother would have been so proud. Cheryl Leaf was never a jealous person. She clearly wanted others to succeed and was always happy when they did. It didn't matter if you were related to her or not—her admiration for hard work and success was not limited to her family.

I try every day of my life to be like her: to love life, love others, and only want the best for everyone. Sometimes it is hard, and other times it is easy. But believing in others doesn't mean that you don't believe in yourself. Being loving and supportive doesn't cost you anything—and in fact, it provides its own sort of "payback."

My grandmother still speaks to me everyday. I try to emulate her love of life, her love of other people, and her welcoming personality.

I thought it was really neat that my 25-cent find sold for about $14, or 64 times what I paid for it. It was shipped to Japan. Crazy that something bought in my little home town and originally made in Sweden is now living in Japan...and even crazier, that I was in an article in *Good Housekeeping!!!!*

#14 Ivory Knife Handle

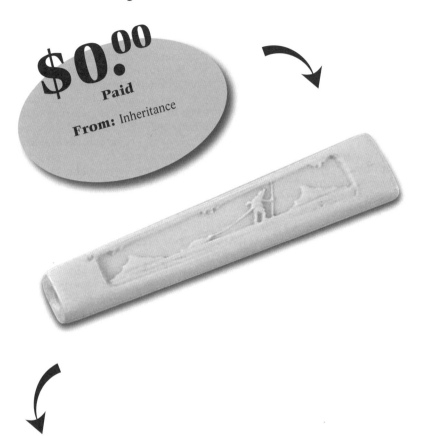

$0.⁰⁰ Paid

From: Inheritance

Ivory Knife Handle Eskimo Native American Hunter Seal

Description:
Neat ivory knife handle looks like it has been carved with a hunter and a seal. Vintage and a great piece in very good condition. I would guess 1940s to 1960s. ½" by 4¹⁄₁₆".

Winning Bid:

$35.⁵⁰

Ended: 9/13/06
History: 4 bids
Starting Bid: $9.99
Winner: Bremerton, WA

Viewed

000057 X

Ivory Knife Handle #14

The Story

This was an item that I inherited from my grandmother's antiques store. My grandmother loved ivory, and it was her dream to one day own an antique carved tusk. My grandmother's dreams revolved around travel and her collections.

My grandma probably owned at least 50 to 60 of these knife handles over the years, and they were strictly to be sold in the antique shop and not to be collected—although I suppose we could argue that just owning 50 of anything constitutes a collection!

Most of these ivory handles walked right in through the front door. That was one of Cheryl Leaf's favorite things to say. If someone would ask her, "Where did you get all this stuff in your store?" she would answer, "Most of it walked right in through the front door." But it was true; every day, at least one person (if not more) would walk up those front steps and set something on the counter to sell. It was a great way to get merchandise, and one reason that I miss having an open shop.

Ivory is different from bone; you can tell real ivory by its tiny cross-hatches. Some people are opposed to reselling ivory because its original source is often animals which are now endangered species. My grandmother would only deal in antique and vintage ivory. She was absolutely opposed to killing living animals for their tusks. In earlier times, however, harvesting ivory was just a way of life.

Ivory is formed from dentine (no, not the chewing gum, but a calcified tissue in the body) and makes up the majority of the teeth and tusks of elephants, hippopotamuses, walruses, and mammoths.

Ivory has been used over the years for many different things. Before the development of plastic, it was used for billiard balls, piano keys, Scottish bagpipes, buttons, and a wide range of other items.

Because of the rapid decline of the elephant population, importing and selling ivory is banned or severely restricted in many countries. Most of the elephant's decline can be traced to poachers prior to the 1980s.

In 2007, eBay accepted the recommendation of the International Fund for Animal Welfare and banned all international sales of ivory products. As of January 1, 2009, eBay expanded this ban so that no ivory whatsoever can be sold on the auction website. I wondered why my ivory auctions had been shut down a few weeks ago, and now because of my research for this story, I know!

Well, I won't be selling any more ivory pieces on eBay. Kind of a shame, since the ivory I own is definitely vintage or antique. And by the way, my grandmother did buy herself that huge carved antique elephant tusk that she had always dreamed of owning. She kept her ivory collection in a special cabinet along with a little bowl of water so that the ivory would not crack. She appreciated her collection and took very good care of it. Unfortunately, it will now be extremely hard to collect antique ivory.

#15 1938 Art Deco Wall Plaque

Signed 1938 Art Deco Plaster Wall Piece Lady Deer RARE!

Description:

This unique piece is signed with what looks like copyright A and an artist's name. If anyone knows who made it I would appreciate knowing. Also signed with "1938 Made in USA." 19" by 1". A lady in a flowing gown with a deer or fawn. It is a very amazing and large piece of wall decor. The lady I bought it from remembers that her grandmother had it on the wall of her home in the 1930s. As is with cracks, flakes and repair.

Winning Bid:

$39.⁹⁹

Ended: 9/14/06
History: 1 bid (sold in store)
Starting Bid: $39.99
Winners: Florida

Viewed

000073 X

1938 Art Deco Wall Plaque   #15

The Story

This is the weirdest story. But on some level aren't all eBay stories strange? My best friend from high school, Melanie Souve, was visiting from Boston in September of 2006. Early one Saturday morning, I dragged her out to garage sales with me. She is a good friend and knows the drill. We went to a house in Rancho Mirage that looked very familiar. I was thinking, "I have been to a sale here before, I just know it."

As I was walking up the driveway, I spotted a round Art Deco wall plaque. It was then that I realized I had bought the one pictured here from this same lady a few years before. I had paid $10 for it in 2004 and I knew that it was still in my eBay store and had not sold, so I didn't feel compelled to buy the matching one. That was a mistake, as you will soon find out!

I did buy a few other things and we headed on our way. We got back to my house and unloaded Mel's rental SUV, and it was then that she realized she had lost her purse with a ton of cash, all her IDs, credit cards, passport and cell phone. Oh, crap! We figured it must have fallen out of the truck at one of the garage sales we had been to. So we hopped back in the rental and start heading towards Rancho Mirage dialing her cell phone the entire way. We were in a panic!

Finally, a woman answered and said, "Yes, you dropped your purse in the street in front of my house." And of course, it was at the house with the plaque that matched mine! The woman was extremely nice, and there was absolutely nothing missing from Melanie's purse when we picked it up. Here was my second opportunity to purchase the matching plaque, and once again I passed. What a knucklehead!

Four days later, I received two emails from eBay. It turned out I had sold not one, but two Art Deco wall plaques. What? Unfortunately, I only had one and someone had listed the same item twice in my eBay store by mistake. Coincidence? I think not.

The bidder (TropicalDave) who bought the plaque turned out to be super nice and not upset at our mistake. He emailed me to say that he would be using the ONE plaque in his home remodel in Deerfield Beach, Florida. Pretty cool! I wonder how the universe knew that there were two of these and that TropicalDave would be buying two of them—if I had only been smarter!

#16 Wilson Goggles

$20.00 Paid
From: House sale

Wilson Sun Goggles Side Shield Tortoise Antique K1

Description:
These are such neat goggles. They are in great condition, signed "Wilson USA." Faux tortoise shell with side shields. Sun goggles or sunglasses. Patented mar. 26 1912. Comes with the original metal case.

Winning Bid: **$140.50**

Ended: 9/19/06
History: 10 bids
Starting Bid: $9.99
Winner: Kalamazoo, MI

Viewed
 X

Wilson Goggles #16

The Story

Melanie was still in town visiting and we had decided to do a girls' spa day. So Melanie, Maureen (Mo), and I started driving towards Desert Hot Springs. There is a spa at the top of Palm Drive that has been there since the 1950's. It is really kitschy, inexpensive, and tucked way far away in what seems like Timbuktu.

As I write this story, it is February of 2009 and Melanie is coming to visit next week. I haven't seen her in two years and she suggested we do another spa day, so I just got off the phone with the Desert Hot Springs Spa to make our reservations. Strange, but true.

But back to September of 2006, as we made our way to DHS, we decided to stop off at a house sale in Cathedral City. Big mistake or not? The people were selling their entire household and moving into an RV. They had a complete set of antique Haviland, tons of Harley items, and a lot of cooking gadgets and chef's tools.

For $700, I bought the set of Haviland, along with some other antique items that were on the floor in the living room. It is always strange to go into someone's home to look at what they have to sell, but sometimes you just have to grin and bear it. These goggles were part of that antique bunch of stuff. They ended up costing me $20.

We quickly packed up everything, put it in the SUV, and told the couple that we would stop back after our spa treatments. The spa day was fantastic, and after our treatments, we ate lunch at the spa's cafe and had a few cocktails.

That was probably my big mistake right there!

When we returned to the house in Cathedral City, I ended up buying not only all the Harley items, the chef tools, and everything that was left, but also an Alfa Romeo convertible. I paid $3,000 for the car because I just knew I could make a quick $1,000 with it. You will have to wait until story #36 to see how this one plays out! But here is a hint: stick to the knitting. What this means is that you should sell only those things that you know the most about.

These goggles, however, turned out to be a huge hit. I did some research on eBay and PriceMiner. I found some important key words, such as "side shields," to use in the title. I looked up values on PriceMiner and noted that Wilson goggles sold for an average of $39.53.

I think these goggles sold for so much more than that because I was also listing a lot of Harley-Davidson items that week. These vintage shades would be awesome for a serious motorcycle enthusiast, and they sold for over $140! The best part was that I got to ship them to Kalamazoo.

I didn't realize that there really was a Kalamazoo. I have heard the phrase "from Timbuktu to Kalamazoo," and now I know that there is a city in Michigan that is named for the Kalamazoo River. Now I just need to find out if there really is a Timbuktu. Or is it located where the Desert Hot Springs spa is?

#17 Harley-Davidson Beer Stein

$5.00 Paid

From: House sale

Evolution V Twin Harley-Davidson Beer Stein FE Cavanagh

Description:
1998 Harley-Davidson Limited Edition First Edition Beer Stein is 10½" by 7". Cavanagh Group by Ceramarte. The engines of Harley-Davidson motorcycles are featured in this series. In great condition. No chips, no cracks, no crazing.

Winning Bid:

$52.00

Ended: 9/19/06
History: 11 bids
Starting Bid: $9.99
Winner: Maine

Viewed
 X

Harley-Davidson Beer Stein #17

The Story

As many of you know, I write a bi-monthly newsletter. It used to be a weekly newsletter, but I found that it was taking up too much time and I needed to focus on helping my Queen's Court members, writing more books, and listing on eBay. If you don't already subscribe to it, please go to www.TheQueenofAuctions.com and sign up now. It's free!

An article I wrote during the time I was listing this beer stein got me into a spot of trouble. I had decided to write about consignment selling as compared to selling for yourself. The fallout shocked me. I got so many hate emails (mostly from consignment sellers), it was insane. It was then that I decided to hire someone else to wade through my inbox and take care of the nasty emails! I take them too personally, and one mean email can ruin my day.

It is funny, because in the two years since I wrote the consignment article, almost all of the consignment chains have gone bankrupt. Here is part of what I wrote. "I am not a big fan of the consignment chains—for several reasons. They only accept relatively big-ticket items (for example, if they don't think your item is worth as much as $50 to $70, they will not put it up for sale for you). They are looking for the easy auctions."

Quite frankly, I don't even know which of my items are $50 items. I never would have picked this stein to be a $50 item. It always shocks me what sells for the most—so I think that the consignment stores are too picky. Also, they take between 25%

and 40% of each sale. That is a lot of money.

I do recommend eBay consignment stores for people who just don't have the time to list on their own. 60% to 75% of an item's value is better than the nothing it would bring by sitting in the closet!

If I had taken this Harley stein into an eBay consignment store, the person behind the counter would have spent ten minutes trying to figure out its value, and would eventually have found that the Evolution Harley beer steins from 1998 typically sell for $18.99 to $34.99. At that point, the clerk would have handed it back to me and said, "Sorry, it doesn't meet our minimum. We can't take it."

I listed it without doing any research, and guess what? It sold for more than any steins in the previous month! One secret of the Dralle Method is that it doesn't require you to spend more than an hour on research each week. "What?" you might be saying. "That goes against everything I've learned." Yes—but my system is proven to work.

Why did this beer stein sell for more than any others? You just never know with eBay. The final auction price really depends on which bidders are in the market for that stein during that particular week. It takes two to tango! And that idiom means that the $52 bid I got for this stein wouldn't have happened without two people competing against each other. And by not reading my hate mail anymore, I have chosen NOT to tango with mean people.

#18 Duster Jacket

$20.00 Paid

From: House sale

Oilskins Outback Duster Riding Jacket Mens XL Like new

Description:
This is a great jacket. Oilskins of the Outback Company Ltd. The Original Bush Outfitters. Made in Costa Rica. Dark brown. Style 2052 Oxford PA. I got a little dust on it when I was taking the pictures but otherwise it is awesome! I bought a bunch of really great Harley-Davidson items and they will all be listed this week.

Winning Bid:

$76.99

Ended: 9/19/06
History: 21 bids
Starting Bid: $9.99
Winner: Ohio

Viewed
 X

Duster Jacket #18

The Story

Funny that a coat from the Original Bush Outfitters would be made in Costa Rica and not Australia. Australia is the one country on my grandmother's list that she never got to visit. She wanted to go there more than anything. Someday soon, I am going to go to Australia for her and scuba dive the Great Barrier Reef.

I remember one Christmas when she was sick and we realized that she would never travel again; we bought her an Australia travel video for a gift. She really appreciated it and she also appreciated the fact that even though she wasn't going to visit in person, that was okay. She never held onto regrets. But I did notice that sometimes (very rarely) she held on to arguments. That was one part of my grandmother that I never did quite understand. I guess we all have our faults, but if you ever crossed her or had a falling out, watch out. She could hold on to a grudge forever.

My grandma had some neighbors, Maude and Gibb Hendry, who were two of her closest friends. They came by frequently, and often brought her dinner. I never did quite figure out what happened between them, but whatever it was resulted in a major falling out. In my naivety, I tried and tried to patch up their friendship. My grandmother would have none of it. My grandmother passed away without ever talking to them again.

I'm still intrigued by that quarrel, and I think about it every time I walk into my office and see a glass jar that my grandmother treasured containing stones from the Mt. St. Helen's eruption. Inside the jar in my G's handwriting is a note which says, "Mt. St. Helens stones thanks to Wonder Boy Hendry." I used to ask her all the time, "What happened that you are still holding such a grudge?" but she would never tell me.

Oh, well, that will be one of life's great mysteries to me. Another one will be that this jacket brand new from the company sells for $99 to $129, and yet I received 77% of that price for it used, despite having only paid $20. You just never know.

But just what is a duster, and why are dusters so desirable? A duster like this keeps you dry and protects you from the elements due to features like a detachable cape that keeps out the wind, rain, and cold. It also has deep cargo pockets and taffeta-lined hand warmers, a tall stand-up collar and double throat latch. These all work to keep warmth in and cold out. I guess you can walk or ride with ease because of the large fantail gusset and double snapped leg straps.

I am thinking that it sold for so much to a Harley rider since I was listing so many other motorcycle items that week. I think that this Australian-inspired duster may have even protected "Wonder Boy Hendry" as he gathered those Mt. St. Helens rocks for my grandmother before their major falling out—or maybe we should call it an eruption!

MT. ST. HELEN'S ROCKS COURTESY OF WONDER BOY HENDRY

#19 Harley-Davidson Saddle Bags

$40.00
Paid
From: House sale

The Leather Works Harley-Davidson Saddlebags WOW Studs

Description:

This is an awesome piece. It is huge and could either be used as a piece of luggage or saddle bags. Each side is 20" by 10" by 12". Has the logo from the Leather Works Store on it. The side is detachable with a zipper. Black leather with silver studs and buffalo head nickels. This is a really neat item. Awesome! In very good to great condition. Could use some leather oil. We have a lot of Harley-Davidson motorcycle items up for sale this week in separate auctions. We bought a super collection.

Winning Bid: $179.00

Ended: 9/21/06
History: 24 bids
Starting Bid: $9.99
Winner: Oregon

Viewed
000254 X

Harley-Davidson Saddle Bags #19

The Story

Finally, I listed a super Harley item that could be used on a real hog. It was fun to list all the Harley items and I learned a lot. I knew absolutely nothing about motorcycles before I bought all this stuff. Mo (Maureen) and her husband Paul used to be really into Harleys, so they helped me out.

Harley-Davidson is a company steeped in American tradition. You have got to love that! The company really began in 1901 when William S. Harley (age 21) drew up plans for a small engine to be used on a pedal bicycle frame. Over the next two years, Harley and his childhood friend Arthur Davidson worked hard on their motor-bicycle. It was finally finished in 1903, but it was unable to conquer the tiny hills of Milwaukee, Wisconsin without pedal assistance.

It was back to the drawing board. The new prototype had a bigger engine and a loop frame design that took it out of the motorized bicycle category and moved it into the motorcycle category, which it would eventually redefine. Congrats to the Americans! The first Harley-Davidson was functional by September 8, 1904, when it competed in a Milwaukee motorcycle race and placed fourth. That would mark the first documented appearance of a Harley-Davidson motorcycle.

The Harley-Davidson company has survived its share of ups and downs over the years. It survived the Depression, built motorcycles for the Army in WWII, had its reputation tarnished through association with the Hell's Angels and other outlaw motorcycle gangs (for whom it was the favored ride), but ended out on top and a favorite of motorcycle enthusiasts the world over.

The man who bought the saddle bags, Ross Kaplan from Portland Oregon, sent me the nicest email when I asked him if he had a special story to tell about this item for my new book. When he bought the saddle bags, he only had eight feedback points by his name. Sometimes we don't like to sell to new eBayers because they can be a lot of trouble—but other times, they can be the best! Ross was one of the best. Here is his email:

Hi Lynn,

Reading your email brought a smile to my face. I love the saddle bags I got from you. A little bit of work and they were as good as new. The buffalo head nickel buttons match the ones on my leather vest. I think the one story about these bags that stands out in my mind was that I found a Leatherman tool in one of the pockets. When I contacted you about sending it back, you said to keep it as a gift. I have used it several times while on the road and camping. Every time, I think of the extra "bonus" that I got with that eBay purchase. Thank you!
Ross

Emails like that make me smile. Thank you, Ross, for being such an awesome new eBayer! We appreciate you.

#20 Akai Reel to Reel Recorder

$15.⁰⁰ Paid

From: House sale

Reel to Reel Tape Recorder Akai GX-4000D Mint in Box

Description:
How often do you see one of these still in the original factory box? Not often. Magnetic tape player by Akai GX 4000D. The box is 16" by 21" by 11". Still in the original factory plastic with the packet of silica gel to keep it fresh. Silver/chrome face with walnut panels. A2UL. Made in Japan. Glass x'tal Ferrite head. The people I bought it from say that it works perfectly and that they took excellent care of it. You can tell by the fact that it is still in its original box.

Winning Bid: **$137.⁵⁰**

Ended: 9/22/06
History: 29 bids
Starting Bid: $9.99
Winner: Toronto, ON

Viewed

000124 X

Akai Reel to Reel Recorder   #20

The Story

I'm sitting in Bellingham, WA at my mom's beach house as I write this. It is February of 2009 and I am in town to celebrate my Dad's 75th birthday. We flew in yesterday and surprised him. He had no clue. I had sent a huge box up to my sister Kiki's house and she and her son Zach decorated it. Her baby Kyle just watched. Then she called my dad as soon as the kids were hidden in the box and said, "Oh my gosh, my sink is leaking and I don't know what to do."

He came running right over with a wrench and flashlight in hand. He was super angry because he had just sat down to watch his favorite team, Gonzaga, play basketball. As he strode through her living room, she said to him, "You have an early birthday present here, would you like to open it?" "NO!" he said. "I am going to fix that leak."

Finally, he came out of the kitchen and said, "There is nothing wrong with your sink" and then he saw Indy sticking out of the box. I don't think we could call the look on his face surprise—it was more like complete and utter shock. He was so happy to see the kids. It was priceless! He kept saying, "Thank you" over and over.

My mom was holding my sister's baby a few minutes ago and she asked, "What story are you working on?" I said, "I am writing about an Akai reel to reel." She said, "That is the baby's name." The baby's name is not "Akai," but rather "Kyle," although everyone calls him "Kai." My sister decided recently to make the change to Kai official. It just seemed so fitting that I should write about this item then.

Kai is eight months old and his brother Zach is almost three years. We hardly get to see them, so we had a great day today playing in the snow at the beach. Tomorrow night is my dad's surprise birthday party. Will the fun never end?

I hope not! I had bought this "a Kai" in that same houseful where I got the Alfa Romeo, and I paid $15 for it.

Reel to reel recorders were the precursors to the cassette; the magnetic tape is exposed as opposed to being enclosed in a cassette (or enclosed in a huge box as a surprise). The reel to reel format was used in the very first tape recorders as far back as the 1930s. Originally this format had no name, but when cassettes were developed in the 1960s, a name was needed to differentiate one from the other. The name "reel to reel" is what is known as a retronym.

I loved learning what a retronym is. A retronym is when the original name of an object must be modified to differentiate it from a newer version of a similar thing. So when cassettes became the rage in the 1960s, the original magnetic tape recorders had to be renamed "reel to reels." Pretty cool.

It was awesome when this retronym sold for $122.50 more than I paid for it . I don't think we could have gotten my dad a better 75th birthday present than just being here in Bellingham to celebrate with him. I am also thinking that Kyle's new name of Kai could also be termed a retronym—although we don't have a new version of him—just a new, better name!

#21 Mandoline

$10.\!^{00}$
Paid
From: House sale

Bron Coucke MIB Original Mandoline Mandolin France PRO

Description:
Professional quality. The box is 16" by 3" by 5½". Original box and still in the plastic. Never used! A very expensive piece originally. Made in France. The original mandoline for cutting food in various and clever ways. Style is 20638. Very high quality and in perfect condition. We have a lot of professional chef tools up for sale this week in separate auctions from two professional executive chefs.

Winning Bid:

$103.\!^{83}$

Ended: 9/23/06
History: 20 bids
Starting Bid: $9.99
Winner: New York, NY

Viewed
000372 X

Mandoline #21

The Story

For those of you who know me already (and for those of you getting to know me), you may have realized that I don't like to cook, nor am I very good at it. I think if I had been a stay-at-home mom (instead of the single mom who has to pay all the bills), I may have learned to enjoy cooking—but I never would have LOVED it. Dinner time at our house is like this: "What can I grab that is healthy and only takes five minutes to prepare?" More often than not, it is salads at the Wendy's drive-through.

Oh, well, Houston is turning into quite the little chef. He follows in his dad's, Mor-Mor's, and Papa's footsteps on this one. I can take no credit. Houston's dad and my parents are awesome cooks and have passed these skills on to Houston—so luckily, we do have one good cook on the premises. Houston will ask me to bring home fresh ingredients like lettuce, vegetables, and meat, and the next thing you know—we have a family dinner!

Because of my cooking history, it was quite strange for me to purchase all the professional chef's tools from the same couple that had all the Harley items in their house sale. They had both been executive chefs and they told me that their pieces were quite amazing. I never quite believe any seller so took all they told me with a grain of salt. Yes, Houston does use some grains of salt and pepper when he cooks also!

I paid $10 for this piece and the cool part was that it had never been used. It is always great to get something mint in the original plastic. When I bought it, I thought a mandoline was a musical instrument. Not!

It turns out that a mandoline is a tool used for slicing and cutting juliennes (long thin strips) and with the proper attachments it can make crinkle cuts (I know what that is from crinkle-cut French fries). One advantage to using a mandoline is that the slices will be uniform in thickness, which is important with foods that are deep fried or baked. It can also be used to slice very, very thin items that would be dangerous to cut using a knife.

The maker of my mandoline was Bron-Coucke. Jean Bron decided in 1950 to manufacture a manual vegetable slicer in steel at the request of professional chefs (to replace the existing wooden models). The mandoline was born. All professional kitchens in the world know the Bron mandoline. In 1975, the company was bought by Andre Coucke. That is why my mandoline was not from the Bron company, but was a Bron-Coucke.

I was ecstatic when my $10 purchase turned into more than $100 on eBay. It made me think more about my dislike of cooking. I almost think that great chefs and cooks (like Houston) are not made, but born. The mandoline was born in 1950—but *my* little chef was born in 1996.

#22 Le Creuset Dutch Oven

Le Creuset Dutch Oven 22 Vintage RARE Blue Fleur de Lis

Description:
This piece is not signed with "Le Creuset," but says "Descoware" (typical of how they marked their goods). I believe that this is an early vintage mark. 22 on the base. The shape is a Dutch Oven with enamel over cast iron with blue fleur de lis design. I have never seen this pattern. Holds about 2 quarts. Some wear and nicks as is common. Looks French Country to me.

Winning Bid:

$51.00

Ended: 9/24/06
History: 6 bids
Starting Bid: $9.99
Winner: Snohomish, WA

Viewed
 X

Le Creuset Dutch Oven #22

The Story

I had a different cookware item picked for this story—a tart ring. I stared at my computer screen for half an hour. I had no inspiration. So I started looking at other items.

When I pulled the file for this item, I realized that this pan had a "22" on the base. AND it was story #22, and 22 is my favorite number, and Houston wears 22 on his baseball team. What do you guys think? I think I made the right choice.

I bought this pan at an estate sale here in the desert and paid $6 for it. Never overlook enameled cookware, especially those pieces made in Europe that are in good condition.

So what is Descoware and Le Creuset? It turns out that my listing was completely incorrect. Today, on eBay, this auction would have probably been shut down for key word spamming. Key word spamming is when you put a word in the title that is a popular search term but doesn't apply to your item. My pan, which was signed "Descoware," was not Le Creuset at all. It was Descoware.

Descoware was a brand of enamel cookware that was the signature brand of Julia Child. It was featured regularly on her show during the 1960s. Now, you all know I wasn't very old in the 1960s and that I definitely wasn't watching THAT show! Did you know that Julia Child was 6' 2"?

Descoware was manufactured in Oudenaarde, Belgium and then imported to the United States beginning in the mid-1940s; it was originally called "Bruxelles Ware." In the 1950s, the D.E. Sanford Company (D.E.S. Co.) took over the business, and thus the name "Descoware" was born.

The gradient red to orange "Flame" pattern was one of their trademark lines. I have sold these pieces before, but they never did quite as well as this blue fleur de lis piece did.

By the mid 1970s, Descoware's competitor Le Creuset had developed such an aggressive marketing campaign that Descoware was in financial ruin. Even though top chefs such as Julia Child rated Descoware ahead of Le Creuset for its functionality, fashion-forward Americans preferred the color variety and trendy designer looks that Le Creuset offered.

In the late 1970s, Le Creuset bought the Descoware trademark and rights. With those patents in hand, Le Creuset continued to use the Descoware (Glissemaille) hard coating and also used the flame coloration for a while (although they don't anymore).

So my listing wasn't completely wrong. Le Creuset did at one time own the Descoware patents, so maybe that is why my listing survived. My neat pan sold for $51 and now I know that I should have put "Descoware" in the title. I may have gotten even more for it if I had, because it turns out that there is a huge fan base for Descoware and for Julia Child.

I am just hoping that Houston gets to be at least as tall as Julia Child's 6'2". His doctor estimated his height to one day reach 6' 4". If he does grow that big, I hope to see

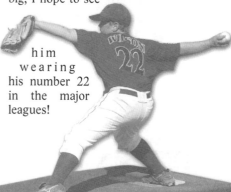

him wearing his number 22 in the major leagues!

#23 Bunny Rabbit Lamp

$15.00
Paid
From: Garage sale

Table Lamp Enamel Bunny Rabbit Asian Cat Blue Colorful

Description:

17.5" tall to the harp and the bunny is about 9" long. Blue, green, pink, yellow. In great condition. Ceramic/enamel with a wooden base. The finial is figural and in the shape of an Asian figure. Reminds me of Tommy Bahama.

Winning Bid: **$100.00**

Ended: 9/24/06
History: 17 bids
Starting Bid: $9.99
Winner: Los Angeles, CA

Viewed
 X

Bunny Rabbit Lamp #23

The Story

It was September and back-to-school was in full swing. Unfortunately, the city redid the school boundary lines in Palm Desert, and my kids were going to have to change elementary schools. What a nightmare!

Houston was going into fourth grade and Indy into second grade. They had both spent their entire school experience at Carter Elementary—and now we had to change. Not cool. I tried everything I could to keep them at Carter. I wrote letters and pled with school officials, but they would not budge for anyone.

So off to the new elementary we went. When we first moved into our house, the school was just one large field. There were many rabbits that lived in that field. Rabbits are small mammals that burrow and are found in several parts of the world—including my part!

The good news was that the new school was very close to our home. Going there actually turned out to be a blessing, as it shaved about 1½ hours of driving off of my day.

I am always harping about lamps being great sellers (harping—get it?). Lamps have harps. That is the part that goes from the neck of the lamp up to hold the shade. And I am a big fan of all animal collectibles, especially rabbits.

I could tell that this rabbit lamp was Asian. I didn't think the work was fine enough to be Japanese, and my gut instinct told me that it was a Chinese import. I also knew that it wasn't cloisonné, as there were no metal wires showing. It was just plain enamel.

Interestingly enough, the rabbit is the fourth animal in the twelve-year cycle of the Chinese zodiac. So, every twelve years it is known as the Year of the Rabbit. According to traditional Chinese astrology, people born in the Year of the Rabbit are articulate, talented, and ambitious, and they possess excellent taste. Rabbit people are admired, trusted, and are often financially lucky, which is why people carry faux rabbit's feet for good luck. It is no wonder that any rabbit item is quite collectible.

When I list a rabbit item, I usually try to get "bunny rabbit" in the title also. This rabbit lamp cost me $15 at a garage sale and never in my wildest dreams would I have thought there would be a bidding war and it would sell for $100 even.

And, our hopping from Carter elementary to the new one actually turned out to be a lucky move as I could now drop off and pick up my kids in about fifteen minutes total per day as opposed to the one hour and 45 minutes it used to take.

I also learned that I was born in the year of the rabbit (I will not share my particular year, but the next year of the rabbit will be in 2011). So maybe my "excellent taste" according to Chinese astrology is what prompted me to buy this winner and make me "financially lucky"!

#24 Cowboy Boots

$20.⁰⁰
Paid
From: Garage sale

Laramie Handmade Leather Boots Mens 10.5 Patchwork

Description:
These boots are vintage and so neat. Brown, black, beige, ivory and buff. I would guess 1970s and the man I bought them from told me that they are a 10½. I did not see a size marked. Style 839 25445. In good used condition. Some wear on the heel.

Winning Bid:

$76.⁰⁰

Ended: 10/3/06
History: 8 bids
Starting Bid: $9.99
Winner: Texas (no kidding!)

Viewed

 X

Cowboy Boots #24

The Story

When Peter and I were in Sonoma a few months prior, he decided he wanted to buy some cowboy boots. He picked up a black pair on that trip.

So when I was out garage saling and saw these (in his size), I thought it was worth $20 to see if the style appealed to Peter. When I got them home and emailed him a photo, we both agreed they were a little wild for him! He is more conservative than that. On to eBay they went.

Cowboy boots sell well on eBay. The history of cowboy boots is quite interesting. According to legend, they originated from a shoemaker in either Kansas or Texas. After the Civil War ended in 1865, the men who drove cattle across the country realized that they needed different boots than those they had worn during the war, since the war boots did not protect them on their long rides.

Around 1870, a very smart cowboy took his war boots to a shoemaker and asked for a pointy toe (to get his foot into the stirrup easily), a taller legging (to protect his legs), and a bigger, thicker, heel. The knee-high design would protect the cowboy from tree thorns, barbed wire, snakes, and other perils.

The higher, underslung heel of the boot also helped the cowboy when he needed to dig into the ground when pulling a stubborn mule or leading a horse down a steep trail. The heel also kept the cowboy's foot from pushing through the stirrup so that if he were thrown from his horse he wouldn't get stuck in the stirrup and drug to death.

Speaking of being drug to death reminded me of a terrible thing that happened to my grandma in the late 1980s. She was in her van at the Alberston's grocery store and started to put her vehicle in park with the door open and the motor running. Instead of going into park, it got stuck in drive, and she fell partially out of the passenger door and was dragged clear across a major shopping center until her van hit a mail box. Luckily, she wasn't killed, but she did break both her arms.

The incident in question was written up in the Bellingham Herald and my grandmother proudly displayed the article on her bulletin board. My grandmother called herself a fighter and was proud of being an overcomer (much like the cowboys in the late 1800s).

The first pairs of cowboy boots had very little style and were intended strictly to provide protection from the many hazards cowboys faced—including being dragged, as my grandma was! These early cowboy boots quickly became a big part of all cowboy's lives. Today, the more elaborate the design the better, as cowboy boots have become quite the fashion statement.

Who would have thought that this pair of stylish 1970s boots would sell for $76 and go back to Texas, where cowboy boots may have originated?

78-Year-Old Woman Dragged by Van

JOHN ADAMS
Herald Staff Reporter

A local woman was dragged by her 1978 Chevrolet van at the Albertsons Shopping Center on Northwest Ave. in Bellingham on Tuesday morning. She was exiting the vehicle when her purse strap caught on the gear shift and sent the van from park into drive.

The van plowed over several medians before hitting a mailbox and coming to a stop. The woman is expected to make a complete recovery and only suffered two broken arms.

#25 Victorian Locket

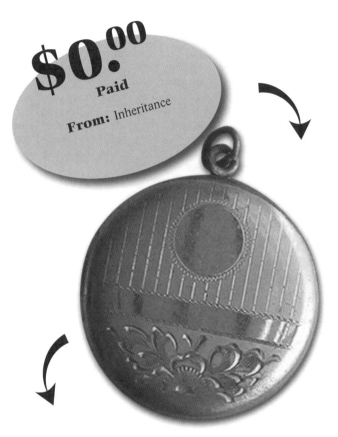

$0.⁰⁰
Paid
From: Inheritance

Victorian Locket Round Gold Filled Antique Floral Lines

Description:
Victorian locket is round. The front of the locket is engraved with flowers and lines. 1". 1890s or so. Some wear. Opens and will hold two photos. We have a lot of neat antique jewelry up for sale this week. My brother is GIA (Gemological Institute of America) certified and he has checked most pieces for us. Bid with confidence.

Winning Bid:

$59.⁹⁹

Ended: 10/17/06
History: 14 bids
Starting Bid: $9.99
Winner: Austin, TX

Viewed
 **X**

Victorian Locket   #25

The Story

This was in a box of things that I inherited from my grandmother. It had been marked $35 in our antique store. That means that right before we shut the doors, it could have been purchased for $10.50 (at 70% off). Someone passed up a bargain.

This locket was gold filled, which means it didn't contain enough actual gold to be called real gold. It would also hold two photos. What are lockets and why were they so popular in antique times?

A locket is a pendant that opens up to hold either a photograph or lock of hair (although the name comes from the French word meaning "to lock," not the English "lock," for a piece of hair). Lockets are typically given to loved ones for special occasions like birthdays. They are also given for weddings, christenings, and were a common funeral gift during the Victorian era.

The locket that I sold definitely looked to be from the late 1800s to me, so I was confident dating it Victorian. The Victorian Era lasted during Queen Victoria of England's reign, from June of 1837 to January of 1901. She held power for almost 64 years.

The Victorian era was a long period of prosperity for the British. This was also the time when a middle class began to develop.

Queen Victoria married her first cousin, Prince Albert, on February 10, 1840. Interestingly enough, she proposed to him! They had nine children together. Although he didn't have much official power, he was involved in many notable issues, including the fight to abolish slavery.

In 1861, at the young age of 42, Prince Albert passed away and Queen Victoria went into a period of mourning that lasted for the rest of her life (40 more years). She refused to go out in public for many years, and when she did, she wore a widow's bonnet instead of her crown.

I think this is when lockets really rose to prominence as a funeral gift. The dearly departed would be remembered with a picture or a lock of hair placed into a locket and then given as a gift. I hope this locket that sold for almost $60 was given for a happy occasion, because it is always amazingly sad for me when I see a locket with someone's photo and hair still inside.

I just went to my china cabinets and pulled out a watch (also gold filled) that my grandmother gave me many years ago. It had belonged to her mother, Maybelle, who passed away April 4, 1913 at the age of 35 when my grandmother was only eighteen months old.

It is engraved with "Mabel" (there was not enough room to spell her name correctly) "from Papa" (her dad) "May 3rd, 1899"—Maybelle's 21st birthday. When Maybelle passed away, my great-grandfather, George, had placed her photo inside her watch (rather than a locket) and he carried that watch in his pocket until his death. It was worn, and you could tell how much he missed and loved her. You could also call a pocket watch a type of locket—yet for a man. As I explained this story and showed the pocket watch to my son Houston, we both teared up.

#26 Huge Head Vase

$10.00
Paid
From: Thrift store

RARE Huge Italy LG Majolica Head Vase Headvase AWESOME

Description:
This wonderful oversized head vase is signed with "LG" or "TG." 12.5" by 16.5" by 7.5". Blue eyes, bust and head vase. There are no chips, but there is a crack in the forehead that I have shown in the photo. Vintage and so much fun.

Winning Bid:

$39.99

Ended: 10/20/06
History: 1 bid (sold in store)
Starting Bid: $39.99
Winner: Mississippi

Viewed
000155 X

Huge Head Vase #26

The Story

I was early to pick up my kids from school so I stopped by one of my favorite thrift stores. I had seen this awesome head vase in the front of the store for several weeks priced at $20 and marked "as is." In the antiques business, marking an item "as is" alerts prospective buyers to the fact that an item has a flaw which might affect its value. The flaw in the case of this head vase was pretty obvious—a tiny hole right between the eyes that had turned into a crack. It looked like she had been shot between the eyes, giving her a kind of wild-eyed stare.

Well, on that particular day, the thrift store had decided to mark the head vase down to $10. Head vases can sell for hundreds, if not thousands, of dollars. Mine didn't go that high, and didn't even sell for $9.99 at auction. So I priced it at $39.99 in my eBay store and it sold exactly two weeks later. I do that a lot. If no one is smart enough to buy an item at auction cheaply, I will raise the price to what I think it is worth and let it sit for a while.

The head vases that sell in the hundreds or thousands range are not huge head vases like mine was. They are the

figural lady head vases that were originally used by florists and were quite popular from the 1940s to 1970s. They came with either a glossy glaze or matte finish. Some were signed, but many came with only a paper label (which is often missing). Because of this, not being able to identify the maker of a head vase is not as much of a problem as it is for other items. Also, well-informed collectors (and there are a lot of them!) can easily identify makers.

The vases ranged from 4" to 7" in height, and the bigger ones typically sell for the most. I guess my head vase at 16 .5" tall was just a little too big! Many head vases were made in Japan (Napco, Enesco, Lefton, Relpo) for import to the U.S., and some were manufactured in the U.S. The ones made in the U.S. tend to be of higher quality, and are therefore more collectible.

Remember, subject matter is often more important than maker in determining market value, and items featuring famous ladies like Jackie O. and Marilyn Monroe can bring in huge money. A Marilyn Monroe head vase by Relpo sold recently for $2,625. Yikes! I hope you all start looking for head vases, but in all my years of being in the antique business, I have only ever found two. I think most people know how collectible they are.

Anyway, to crack my kids up (since my head vase was already cracked), I put the vase in the back seat and buckled her in. She was that huge. When I picked my kids up from school, they laughed so hard that of course we had to take photos. You just never know when you will need one for a book you are writing!

#27 Daum Cat

$25.00
Paid

From: Community garage sale

Daum France Art Glass Crystal Large Kitty Cat Signed !!

Description:
Nice piece is signed near the base in etching with "Daum France."
In excellent condition. Clear art glass crystal. 10" by 4" by 3.5". A
fairly heavy and substantial piece.

Winning Bid: **$127.**50

Ended: 10/29/06
History: 10 bids
Starting Bid: $49.99
Winner: Houston, TX

Viewed

000101 X

The Story

It was almost Halloween when I found this cat at a community garage sale. It was signed "Daum France," but had a $45 price tag on it. Give me a break. I said, "I really like this item, but it is out of my price range. Would you take any less?"

"How about $25?" Sold! I didn't know if it was from the same Daum Nancy company that made the art glass my grandmother had collected or not. But it was a substantial piece with a French signature. I knew I could at least get my $25 back, and maybe more. I like trying different items on eBay. I am a risk taker, and I think taking risks is the best way to learn.

I listed the cat without doing any research. I was excited when it sold for $127.50 right around Halloween. When I started writing this story, I finally did more research.

It did turn out that this "Daum France" company was the same as the "Daum Nancy" that produced the cameo glass my grandma collected. The Daum family were originally lawyers, not glassmakers. But they entered the glass making world when Jean Daum acquired a glassworks in Nancy in 1878 as partial payment of a debt.

Daum began making window glass and glassware for taverns. In 1889, his two sons, Auguste and Antonin, saw the Art Nouveau cameo glass by Emile Galle at the Paris Exhibition, and it made a huge impression on them. The Daum brothers were well known for taking calculated risks, and they jumped head-first into the cameo glass business.

There were four major eras of Daum glass. The first era was Art Nouveau, which lasted from 1891 to 1920 and included cameo glass, enameling, acid etching and engraving. Very expensive and still collectible today.

Next came Art Deco, from 1920 to about 1940. Paul Daum, the son of Auguste, designed bowls and vases with geometric patterns on thick glass.

During the third era, the company produced free forms in crystal, and (after 1945) heavy leaded crystal figurines, and serving pieces. This period, during which my cat appeared to have been made, continued until the late sixties.

Finally, around 1968, the fourth (and current) era began, and the company's focus shifted to a production process in which finely crushed glass is mixed with a binding agent to make a paste. Then the paste is coated onto the inside of a negative mold and fired. Daum, now known as "Cristallerie Daum," also hired famous designers (such as Salvador Dali and Paloma Picasso) to contribute to their lines.

As this was selling, my kids asked me to take them for pedicures—Houston's first and Indy's third—because they wanted crazy toenails for Halloween. Indy chose pink polish to match her hand-made Hannah Montana costume (which I bought on eBay) and Houston wanted red toes to match his USC Trojan costume. I guess my children are risk takers also, and don't care what people think about them.

And the Daum cat profit covered (just barely) the $50 Hannah costume and the $45 Trojan costume. Yikes!

#28 Asian Drug Tools

$0.⁰⁰
Paid

From: Inheritance

Antique Asian Ethnic Chatelaine Drug Spoon Pick Tweezer

Description:
This very interesting piece is from about 1900. It is 1" by 6". Silver colored metal. Asian or ethnic Afghani tribal. Like a chatelaine that would have held tools for sewing—I think that this holds tools to use for drugs. Drug paraphernalia. There is a spoon, a pick and what looks like tweezers. Very ornate and hand-made. A unique and interesting piece no matter what it is for.

Winning Bid:

$41.⁰⁰

Ended: 10/30/06
History: 3 bids
Starting Bid: $24.99
Winner: Tokyo, Japan

Viewed
000037 X

Asian Drug Tools #28

The Story

Wow, this crazy thing was in one of my inherited boxes from the shop. I was listing inventory that I already owned because I was rapidly trying to get ready for my last Live Boot Camp of 2006. Yes, that was the year I did three Live Boot Camps and vowed to never do more than one per year again. This Boot Camp was in November near Los Angeles Airport.

Many of you have asked me to hold Live Boot Camps in other parts of the country, and I wish that I could, but after the Bellingham and LA ones in 2006, I realized it would be too much for me. Here are the challenges. I bring the 100 items that I will be listing that week, as well as screens and projectors I use for my talks. I also brought 700 items that had never been listed on eBay to the LA Boot Camp for my students to choose from in a faux garage sale.

A faux garage sale? Yes, I gave each of my students faux money and they got to pick items to list and sell on eBay. Elizabeth bought the best item for ten fake dollars—an Asian (Japanese) cloisonné vase that ended up going for $330! Pretty cool.

I guess I had Asian items on my mind as I packed for Live Boot Camp and listed this item on eBay. I thought it could either be Asian or Afghani tribal, and suspected it had been used in the drug trade somehow.

It turns out that I was right about it being Asian, but wrong about it being drug paraphernalia. What a great word. "Paraphernalia" can mean the miscellaneous gear required for a particular operation or sport.

I also thought it resembled a chatelaine, which is a decorative belt hook worn at the waist with chains suspended from it. Chatelaines were used before pockets were common, and small household items such as, scissors, thimbles, watches, keys and so on, were hung from them.

To solve the mystery, I spent a lot of time researching this piece on the Internet, but kept coming up empty-handed. Finally, I was fortunate enough to stumble across the web site of Silva at www.oldbeads.com. She is amazingly knowledgeable. I emailed her a photo, and she knew exactly what it was. It turns out that I was right about it being Asian—Chinese, in fact—but way wrong about it being drug paraphernalia. Here is some of what she told me:

> It certainly looks Chinese and could be 50 years old. It is a tool kit and with tribal jewelry the pendant parts typically have symbolic meanings with references that have been passed on through generations. Most of the meanings have to do with health, wealth, good relations etc.

How cool is that info? This piece sold for $41 and was shipped to Japan (Asia on my mind again). It did in fact turn out to be a type of paraphernalia—a toolkit for a nomadic tribe. There is a lot of paraphernalia required to hold a Live Boot Camp and that is why those Boot Camps are staying close to my home! They will NOT become nomadic. Boot Camp in a Box, however, *is* nomadic and will come right to your house. To learn more, visit BootCampBox.com

#29 Ferrandiz Wedding Plate

$8.00/4
Paid
From: Church sale

1973 Wedding Day Plate Children Juan Ferrandiz Anri

Description:
Wedding day collector's plate designed by Juan Ferrandiz for Anri 9". In very good condition. Darling children. We have more Anri plates up for sale in separate auctions this week. No box and no COA.

Winning Bid:

$71.48/4
Ended: 11/10/06
History: 13 bids/4
Starting Bid: $9.99 ea auction
Winner: South Korea

Viewed
 X

Ferrandiz Wedding Plate   #29

The Story

I was at the Fire House charity sale which is held around Halloween, and is usually awesome. This sale is where I bought the Baccarat Chandelier from *Money Making Madness* story #57 that sold for over $2,000. I always have high hopes at that sale.

There wasn't much this time. I did find some Anri wood collector's plates in the boutique area. They were marked $4 each, and on the last day of the sale I got them for half price, so I paid $8 for four plates. My grandmother (of course) carried Anri in her antique store, so I knew that sometimes these could be good.

Anri is a German company. From 1902 to 1952, all its products were hand-carved in the homes of the carvers. They call it "home work" on their website. How cool is that? The different craftsmen carved traditional German farming figurines and bottle stoppers. Once carved, the artist would sell them to Anri, and an Anri signature was added. The pieces were intricately carved by hand and varied so that they all looked different. I love this line from the website: "Today you may find these at flea markets and in antique stores." And hopefully at garage sales, so we can sell them on eBay and make big bucks!

After 1952, Anri moved its operations from the home-based model into a factory where machines aided the carvers. The quality became more consistent, which enabled Anri to grow—so much so that over 15,000 different items have been created since then.

In the 1970s, Anri jumped into the collector's plate business, and one of their most famous and beloved collector's plate designers was Juan Ferrandiz. Identifying items designed by Ferrandiz can be tricky, because the F in his signature often looks like a J. I buy Ferrandiz items whenever I see them, and three of the Anri plates I bought that day had his signature. The one that sold for the most was a Ferrandiz wedding day plate which went for $38. All four sold for a total of $71.48 and were shipped to South Korea.

Ferrandiz was born in Barcelona, Spain, in 1918. His works focus on the power of love, and the innocence and purity of children. He was the illustrator and author of 55 children's books in Spanish. He was a painter who wrote poetry and a poet who painted pictures. His pictures were turned into wood carvings. His subjects include animals and children and his belief that children are the future of the world shines through in his work. Ferrandiz passed away in 1997 at the age of 79.

The four Anri plates were some of the "paraphernalia" I took with me to the LAX Boot Camp; my mom wrote them up on my *I Sell* sheets in front of the class to help teach my system. I actually listed these plates in the class at 6 pm on our first day, Friday. On Saturday, after our faux garage sale, I had my students list their own items in front of me. Talk about "home work!"

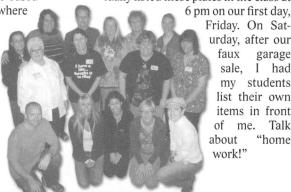

#30 Grateful Dead Beanie Baby

$2.⁵⁰

Paid

From: Ex-husband

Grateful Dead Bean Bear 1st Delilah No Black Paws RARE

Description:

I guess the Delilah with no black paws is rare because not many were made. Bean bear is made by Liquid Blue and is a 1st edition mint with tags. Darling bear is yellow, gold, brown and black leopard print. I have a ton of these Beanie Bean bears up for sale this week. They come from a smoke-free environment. We had a Liquid Blue account at our antiques and gifts store, so these came directly from the company. I just unearthed a huge box full. Don't miss out.

Winning Bid:

$77.⁹⁹

Ended: 11/14/06
History: 37 bids
Starting Bid: $9.99
Winner: Alabama

Viewed

`000092` **X**

Grateful Dead Beanie Baby #30

The Story

I was very grateful and not dead when my third Boot Camp of 2006 was over. What a whirlwind. Time to get back to selling on eBay. When Beanie Babies were hot, we decided to carry the Liquid Blue Grateful Dead bears in the store also. We did this because my husband (at the time) was a Deadhead—a huge fan of the band the Grateful Dead. Many Deadheads even followed the Grateful Dead around the country to see their concerts.

The Grateful Dead started in 1965 in the San Francisco area and became known for their unique style which combined many different types of music, including bluegrass, blues, folk, rock, reggae, country, jazz, gospel and soul. I am surprised they didn't also incorporate opera! In any event, they were a hugely popular band that changed the face of music today.

The Liquid Blue bears sold well in our antiques and gifts store, but not as well as the Ty Beanie Babies. My ex-husband, William, had collected a complete set of all the Dead bears and called me to see if I wanted to buy them. Sure, why not? I will try anything on eBay. I paid him $2.50 for each bear and I think I bought about 60 of them.

It turns out that the best one of the bunch was Delilah, so named for the Samson and Delilah song by the Grateful Dead. Delilah is the woman who cuts Samson's hair in the biblical story, taking away his strength.

Speaking of hair, we had finally gotten Maureen (Mo), my assistant

for two years, to stop wearing her hair in a bun. That was enough of a change for me, but then when this bear was selling, Mo sat me down to tell me that it was time for her to go out on her own and start her own eBay business. I certainly didn't blame her. It eventually happens with most eBay assistants. They figure out that they can make much more money selling on their own. I was very sad, because not only was I losing a great employee, I was also losing the chance to work all day with one of my best friends.

I was grateful for the two years she worked with me, but who was going to ship these darn bears?

Delilah also came with a birth date (6/21/1980) and a birthplace: West High Auditorium in Anchorage, Alaska. I also learned from a nice eBayer that out of the 55,464 Delilah's that were produced before being retired in June of 1998, only 11,040 were made with no paws. What that means (as you can see in the photo) is that Delilah didn't have black material where her paws should be.

Delilah sold for $75 more than I paid for her. Cool! Now, I had to work on replacing Mo. That was going to be very hard to do, because with her unique mixture of wit, sarcasm, humor, empathy, and friendship, along with her amazing work ethic, she helped to change the face of my eBay business, just as the Grateful Dead changed the face of the music world.

#31 Hall Pottery Jockey Ashtray

$6.00
Paid

From: Charity sale

Cast Iron Jockey Ashtray Hall Pottery Vintage Unique!

Description:
This is a very unique piece. 9" by 6½". Signed with a "21" and "Made in USA Hall." Black pottery base with a cast iron jockey. Have never seen one like this. In great condition with some minor nicks.

Winning Bid: **$42.62**

Ended: 11/16/06
History: 8 bids
Starting Bid: $9.99
Winner: Eaton, OH

Viewed

000039 X

Hall Pottery Jockey Ashtray #31

The Story

I got this at a charity sale for $6. This was one item that I picked to research and I couldn't find out anything about it. Today, as I do my research for this story, I found out some amazing information that would have probably doubled my selling price. I think that just adding "NY 21 Club" to the title may have made me an extra $60. But who really knows? Similar items I discovered in my research today all sold for over $100. Darn it!

It turns out that the "21" on the base was for the famous 21 Club in New York City. The first 21 Club was opened in Greenwich Village in 1922 as a speakeasy. A speakeasy was what a bar was called during Prohibition (1919 to 1933), when it was illegal to sell, transport, or manufacture alcohol.

The speakeasy was founded by cousins Jack Kreindler and Charlie Berns. In 1929 it was moved from Greenwich Village to its current location at 21 West 52nd Street and renamed "Jack and Charlie's 21," the "21" obviously being for the street number.

The 21 Club was raided many times during Prohibition, but the club had an amazing set of switches that would tip the bar shelves (and all the liquor) into a chute that fed into the sewer! Cool! Now here is where my ashtray comes into the story.

The bar walls and ceiling are covered with antique toys and sports memorabilia donated by famous patrons. The most notable feature of 21 is the row of hand-painted cast iron jockey statues on the balcony above the entrance. In the 1930s, some of the more wealthy customers showed their appreciation by presenting the club with jockeys painted to represent the racing colors of the stables they owned. There are 33 such jockeys on the exterior and two more inside the front doors.

At Christmas, the regulars (such as Gerald Ford, JFK, Elizabeth Taylor, Mae West and so on) would receive a silk scarf decorated with the club insignia. Each scarf was numbered and had the jockey logo along with a design evoking the famous railings on the building. I want to find one of these scarves—I bet they sell for a lot!

Darn, if I had just been to the 21 Club I would have known that this ashtray was made for them by Hall pottery in the 1940s. Hall Pottery was founded in 1903 in East Liverpool, Ohio. It is most famous for its decorated teapots, and was at one point the world's largest teapot producer. Their teapot line was very famous from 1910 to 1960. Demand dwindled in the 1960s as more people turned to drinking coffee.

Funny that the "tea"totalling (teetotalling—which means abstaining from alcohol) Hall company made the ashtrays for one of the most interesting and famous speakeasies I have ever heard about. Crazy.

#32 Harry Potter Wand

50¢

Paid

From: Garage sale, Birch Bay, WA

Harry Potter Master Wand NIB Alivans COA Wooden Velvet

Description:
Master wand comes with COA (certificate of authenticity), wooden box and red velvet bag. Alivans new in box, master Wandmakers #1872/5000. Limited edition.

Winning Bid:

$16.¹²

Ended: 11/16/06
History: 3 bids
Starting Bid: $9.99
Winner: Attalla, AL

Viewed
 **X**

Harry Potter Wand #32

The Story

I bought this wand at a Birch Bay, Washington, garage sale in the summer, and now that it was three months later, I was just getting around to listing it. Isn't that just the way? Birch Bay is a community (not a city) north of Bellingham. My mom, dad, grandma, great grandmother, great grandfather—basically the entire family—used to love to have picnics on the beach there.

Birch Bay was named by a member of the Vancouver Expedition who used it as an anchorage for several days and named the bay after the birch trees he spotted on the shore. The bay's half-moon shape and calm waters are caused by the refraction of incoming waves on the headlands that lie on either side of the bay. The waves bend as they enter the bay and lose energy in the process.

My dad and his wife (Sue) have a cabin there, and so does my friend Jo Dallas. Every summer we try to do a high school girls' weekend, and this year Jo had offered to host. On Saturday morning of the weekend, I asked the girls if they wanted to go garage saling with me, and quite a few of them jumped at the chance. It was fun. I found this wand on the ground at a garage sale pretty close to Jo's cabin, priced at 50 cents. Why not buy it? It would be easy to ship home, and Harry Potter had just become Houston's favorite series of books to read.

Houston has always been a good reader, but when he got hooked on Harry Potter...watch out! Same with Indiana—they each read an 800-page book in a day. My goodness! I asked them why they loved the Harry Potter books so much.

Indiana told me she loves the books because of the way JK Rowling takes you to a different world. She said she forgets what is happening here, and when she is finished with the book she just wants to go back to that imaginary place.

Houston told me he loves the books for the way the author sets up everything like it is real, and it seems as if she is there, watching the events as they unfold. Houston also likes the magic and violence. Typical boy!

My kids are obviously not alone in their love for Harry Potter. Anything Harry Potter can be collectible and worth a lot on eBay—as long as it wasn't overproduced. This wand was a good bet since it was a limited edition, number 1872 out of only 5000 made, and it was produced by the Alivans company. Alivans wands are handcrafted from a solid block of only the finest hardwoods and are an "official" Harry Potter supplier (very important, readers). But these wands are only to be used for good!

Birch Bay has been nothing but good to my family through the generations and so has eBay. On eBay I made 32 times my investment in one week! Good magic!

#33 Puppy Figurine

$3.00
Paid

From: 'Come see Ben' Estate sale

Puppies Figurine Signed Sun Ray Lladró B & G Spaniels

Description:
Looks like two cocker spaniel puppies to me in muted colors. White, gray and blue. Signed with a sun, tree, and rays or face. Anyone know the maker? We would like to know. In great condition with no chips, no cracks, no crazing.

Winning Bid:

$51.00
Ended: 11/16/06
History: 10 bids
Starting Bid: $9.99
Winner: Prosser, WA

Viewed
 **X**

Puppy Figurine   #33

The Story

I got a phone call one day from a very famous estate dealer out here in the desert named Ben Hegel. Ben's motto was "Come see Ben." He wanted me to know that he was having an estate sale and asked if I would like to come by. The first time I met Ben, he scared me. He's about 6' 6", and a UCLA alum. We didn't quite see eye to eye (literally, since I am 5' 7", and in our choice of colleges). When people asked Ben for a special deal on anything, he let you know that wasn't an option by growling.

Over the years, I came to realize that Ben was really just a big teddy bear and a lovely man. He had a cocker spaniel named Mitzi who followed him everywhere. She was an awesome dog. So, when Ben invited me to this estate sale, I couldn't resist buying this figurine of two spaniel puppies for only $3.

I have never made a ton of money on the things I've bought from Ben. He and his staff (Panos, Bob and Nancy) knew what they were doing and priced their items appropriately; I knew I wouldn't get a real steal, but I did usually double my money. And to get good quality items, it was always worth it to attend one of their sales. So I was very surprised when this figurine sold for more than $50.

What amazes me even more as I write this story is that as I look at my title, I am appalled. This auction would have been shut down so fast on today's eBay. You can not use words in the title like B&G and Lladró if the item up for auction isn't from those companies. Yikes! I was lucky. The figurine did

have the Bing & Grondahl and Lladró look to it, but it wasn't made by either company—and I still don't know who the maker is. Apparently, it didn't matter to the buyer either. Here is a nice email that I got from her...

> I purchased this spaniel for my collection because it reminds me of my search and rescue spaniel 'Murphy.' Murphy is very dear to my heart.

Just remember that dog items, no matter who the maker, sell well because dogs are very dear to their owners and those owners will pay good money for items that remind them of their pets.

Unfortunately, Ben passed away at age 77 from an ongoing battle with cancer. It was very sad, but everyone knew it was inevitable. Strangely enough, the day Ben died, September 11, 2008, is exactly 10 years after I first signed up to sell on eBay, September 11, 1998.

When Ben died, Mitzi went to live with Ben's friend and co-worker Nancy, who has a house two doors down from Ben. The saddest part of this story is that when I went to the estate sale at Ben's house after he passed away, I saw Mitzi coming down the street from her new home at Nancy's place. She walked right into her old house looking for her master. It broke my heart.

#34 Japan Pagoda Earrings

$0.00 Paid
From: Inherited

Carved Crystal Pagoda Earrings Sabino Amazing OLD Japan

Description:
These vintage/antique earrings have clip on tops and are marked "Japan Silver." They are a bluish-green iridescent that reminds me of French Sabino glass. They are 3-sided and carved so that you see a tower pagoda or building from all sides. 1½" long. Amazing.

Winning Bid:

$65.00
Ended: 11/19/06
History: 1 bid (sold in store)
Starting Bid: $65.00
Winner: North Carolina

Viewed
000257 X

Japan Pagoda Earrings   #34

The Story

These were the neatest crystal or glass earrings ever. They completely intrigued me. I inherited them from the antique store, where they had been marked $95. I tried them at auction in July of 2006 at $49.99, and when they didn't sell, I raised the price to $65 and put them in my eBay store. They stayed in my eBay store for only about four months before they sold and were shipped to North Carolina.

I think that they brought in so much because of the beautiful glass and also because of the wonderful pagoda symbol. A pagoda is a unique architectural structure. A true pagoda may only be located on Buddhist Temple grounds.

The Japanese are very particular about how they build their pagodas. The widths of the roofs start out the largest at the base and decrease in size as they approach the sky. The idea is to create ascending lightness that leads up to the heavens. Pagoda carpenters and architects in Japan will only use wood that is at least 1,000 years old; they value the quirks within the wood and work to use it to its best and highest service.

Because they are completely made of wood, pagodas have been extremely vulnerable to fire. Many of these structures were destroyed by fires from either being struck by lightening or destroyed in war. However, because of their interlocking posts and beams, they are extremely resistant to earthquakes and typhoons.

My grandmother was nuts for jewelry, and always had tons of it in the shop. When I had moved back home in 1993 to take care of her, we changed the store layout and moved the jewelry cases from the front to the side. That way we could sit behind the counter and watch the entire shop. We also made the old hallway into a jewelry aisle and opened up the bedrooms in that hallway to the public. We painted them white and put in new carpeting. It really gave us so much extra space. It was awesome.

My mother's old bedroom became the Ty Beanie Baby, Boyds Bear, Yankee Candle and Groovy Girl gift room, and my grandparents' old bedroom became a bead and jewelry room. We put many locked jewelry cases in that back room so that people could browse, but would need a sales person to unlock a case if they needed a closer look.

Leading down that hallway were three huge cabinets that were built into the wall. My grandfather (an architect) had built these at my grandmother's request. I loved to go into them and dig through all the goodies with my grandma. Finally, with so much extra space available, we could get all that merchandise priced and into the shop. It was a huge undertaking, but we did it. Once those cabinets were emptied out, we took off the hinged doors and *voila,* we had some serious sales space.

Those shelves were where we stored these earrings in a locked case. The Japanese took great care in the construction of their pagodas, as did my grandfather when he built the shelves that we used in our antiques business.

#35 Gumps Majolica Villa

$10.⁰⁰
Paid
From: Pallet from Gumps

Gumps Ceramic Villa MIB Majolica Figural Building Italy

Description:
This neat villa is white and is 8" by 8" by 7". In the shape of a building. Majolica. Designed exclusively for Gumps and comes in the original box. Excellent condition.

Winning Bid: **$109.⁵⁰**

Ended: 11/29/06
History: 13 bids
Starting Bid: $9.99
Winner: Virginia

Viewed
 X

Gumps Majolica Villa #35

The Story

We had just cleaned up the eBay room and found this item that I had bought in July of 2005 on a pallet of overstocks from Gumps. We checked on eBay and this villa was NOT listed anywhere.

Well, let's get it listed! I decided that I would start it at $9.99. Nothing to lose. The Gumps items had made me enough profit. I was so excited when this white Italian majolica piece sold for over $100! And the best part was the back story about the buyer.

Here is the email I received:

> The building that I bought from you is very special to me. First, because it is a replica of Palladio's Villa Capra (also known as Rotonda) near Vicenza, Italy. Secondly, I collect porcelain souvenir buildings of real places. So, this villa fits right in with my collection of more than 2,000 buildings. Most of my pieces are much smaller than the one I got from you, so it helps give my display depth.
>
> This Villa Capra was on display when the Souvenir Building Collectors (to which I belong) was here in Charlottesville for their 2008 convention. This group collects metal buildings, so seeing my porcelain collection was definitely mind-expanding for them! Good luck with your book, Elizabeth.

Wow! It just goes to show you that you never know what is collectible and how many different collectibles organizations there are.

But let's learn a little more about Villa Capra. It is a Re-naissance villa just outside of Vicenza in northern Italy. The full name is "Villa Almerico-Capra," and it is also known as "La Rotonda Villa."

It all started out in 1565, when Paolo Almerico (a priest who retired from the Vatican), decided to return to his hometown of Vicenza and build a country house. The site he selected was on a hilltop just outside of the city. The design was for a completely symmetrical building with four facades. "Rotonda" refers to the central circular hall with its dome.

This amazing piece of architecture has been the inspiration for more than a thousand buildings, including part of the White House and Jefferson's home Monticello.

My mom was inspired by her father (an architect) and started drawing home plans when she was just five. She designed the awesome house on Bayside Road where I grew up.

The Villa Capra is currently owned by Mario di Valmarana, a former professor of architecture at the University of Virginia. The villa has been his family's home for more than two centuries. It's funny how Elizabeth, who purchased my model, was employed by the University of Virginia at the time she bought it.

Very circular, all of this eBay stuff! Just like the Rotonda. Rotunda now means "a large circular room with a domed ceiling." And my piece sold for $109.50 on a $10 investment! Round is awesome.

#36 Alfa Romeo Convertible

$3,000.00
Paid
From: Estate sale

1981 Alfa Romeo: Spider Veloce

Description:

I have only owned this for a short time. It is a darling car. Runs fine on city streets but SHOULD NOT be driven on the freeway. I got an inspection at Pep Boys. Oil level and coolant levels are good. There is a transmission leak. Belts and hoses in good condition. Lights all work. Filters are in moderate condition. Brakes are in good condition with 40% remaining. Rear differential leak drain plug. Suspension needs work. Upper strut mount brushing loose. This car is being sold AS IS. It has license tags from 2001 so has not been driven much. I will be happy to fax the car report to anyone who would like to see it. Damage to the bumper, rag top is torn, ding on the side and the driver door handle falls off. Damage to the leather seats. This is a great car and with a little TLC it will be awesome!

Winning Bid: **$2,051.00**

Ended: 11/30/06
History: 2 bids
Starting Bid: $1,995.00
Winner: North Carolina

Viewed
000293 X

Alfa Romeo Convertible #36

The Story

Can you say "mistake?" I certainly can. I had bought this car back in September after a day at the spa with Mo and Melanie. Mo reminded me just the other day that she had wanted to buy it and I had talked her out of it. Lucky her. Stupid me. This is hands down the worst eBay mistake I have ever made, and it cost me at least $1,000.

I thought I could buy this car and turn it very quickly for an extra $1,000. I listed it on eBay in September with a starting bid of $3,995. It did not sell and it would take me two more long months to get a rid of it (my sister says "get a rid of," not "get rid of.")

This was after I took it to Pep Boys and got an auto inspection. The car was a mess, despite the fact that the owners had told me that it was in great condition. Can you say "sucker"?

Anyway, my mom had an Alfa Romeo when I was growing up. It was such a cute little car, and she loved it. She even let me and Hank drive it over to Orcas Island when I was home visiting one summer. I knew that Alfa Romeos have a huge following, and how could this darling car not be worth $4,000? Well, it wasn't. It immediately started leaking oil in my garage. And if I didn't drive it every other day, it wouldn't start.

The kids and I drove it down to the tennis courts often. I was afraid to drive it outside of our gated community on the main roads. The only good thing that came out of this was that we played ALOT of tennis.

The Alfa Romeo company was founded in 1910 in Milan, Italy. The company went through many changes over the years. It began producing race cars, and during WWI (1915) produced military hardware for the war. Also in 1915, Nicola Romeo (a skillful engineer and sports car enthusiast) took over the company, and in 1920 his name was added to make the name "Alfa Romeo."

In 1932, the company was in trouble and the government bailed it out—it became part of Mussolini's Italy. Enzo Ferrari became the head of the race department. Alfa Romeo won many race victories throughout the 1930s. It's said that Henry Ford used to doff his hat when he saw an Alfa Romeo pass.

The Spider Veloce convertible was introduced in 1970, and the traditional rounded tail of the Alfa Romeo was cut off to be more square and yield more luggage space. My Spider was a 1981. These cars were discontinued in 1983. In 1987, Alfa Romeo joined with the Fiat group.

Alfa Romeo introduced many cars over the years: their expensive cars gave way to sporty cars, which in turn gave way to affordable cars. The Alfa has always been an object of desire, a status symbol and an image of beauty and Italian style. How can that have translated into a $1,000 loss? Can you say, "Never buy a car that you know nothing about?" I certainly can—now.

#37 Annalee Santa and Mrs. Claus

$10.^{00}/2
Paid
From: Garage sale

Annalee Thorndike Super Big Mrs Santa Claus 1991 NEAT

Description:
Awesome. We have the matching Mr. Santa Claus also up for sale this week in a separate auction. Needs a slight cleaning. The stand needs repair—it is wobbly. Still in great condition. Huge and 33" tall. Still has the original price tag from May Company for $190.00.

Winning Bid:

$88.^{50}/2

Ended: 12/1/06
History: 14 bids/2
Starting Bid: $9.99 ea
Winner: Harpers Ferry, WV

Viewed
 **X**

Annalee Santa and Mrs. Claus #37

The Story

I sold these Annalee dolls a week after Thanksgiving in 2006. It was a pretty sad Thanksgiving for us because my mom wasn't in town, so my brother didn't come out from LA. It turned out to be just me and my kids. At least I have awesome kids! We decided that since no one was in town, except for us, we would do the 5K Turkey Trot on El Paseo.

We survived. We walked and ran it and finished in about 44 minutes. It was a blast and afterwards I took the kids to Sherman's Deli for breakfast; they had the hugest waffles on the menu with whipped cream and jam. They deserved it. For dinner we had Carl's Jr. drive-through cheeseburgers. What a strange Thanksgiving.

Speaking of strange, these were two strange yet darling Annalee dolls that I had bought at a garage sale before Thanksgiving. When I saw the May Co. price tag for $190 on the Mrs. Claus, it brought back memories. I was an executive trainee, department manager, and eventually a buyer for May department stores. I knew that I had to buy these dolls. They were priced at $10 each, but I asked if they would take less. The sellers agreed to $10 for both. Done deal!

Annalee Thorndike's dolls are very easy to spot. The style is all her own. You may have even seen them around but not known to buy them. S. B. Annalee Davis Thorndike was born in 1915 in New Hampshire. In the 1930s she made her first dolls by dying felt, forming it into dolls, and then painting faces on her creations.

Annalee married, and she and her husband Chip Thorndike lived on a chicken farm in New Hampshire. When the farm went belly-up in the 1950s,

Annalee had to take her childhood hobby and turn it into a real business. And boy, did she!

Let's stop for a moment and figure out what "belly-up" means. Wow, that expression is actually in the Miriam Webster dictionary, which says it means "given up, defeated or bankrupt." Its origin is from the position a fish assumes when it dies.

Back to Annalee. The chicken coop became her workroom, Chip her salesman, and Annalee the designer. Annalee's dolls were usually fashioned after her two sons, who were always involved in some form of activity, whether it was ice skating, skiing, or sledding.

The 1980s brought the focus of the company to Christmas and other holidays. I wonder if it has a Thanksgiving doll? I bet it does. The company became a huge success and it believes that success is based on Annalee's sense of humor and the upbeat looks on the dolls' faces. When you look at these smiles, you just have to smile back. Annalee passed away in 2002 at the age of 87, but the company continues on.

The Mrs. Claus sold for more than Mr. Claus ($52.50 to his $36), probably because I was missing my mom and her amazing home-cooked turkey dinner. It would have been nice to belly up to   my mom's dinner table that day!

#38 Boyds Bear

$2.00
Paid
From: Ex-husband

Boyds Bears Retired Teddy Bear Bean Bag White 1985 Cute

Description:
This is a darling Boyds Bear Bean Bag Teddy Bear from 1985. Originally copyrighted in 1985, it is marked "Boyds Collection Ltd. Hand made in China." White with a red bow. About 12" tall. In great condition from a smoke free home.

Winning Bid: **$54.⁷⁸**

Ended: 12/1/06
History: 4 bids
Starting Bid: $9.99
Winner: Gilroy, CA

Viewed
 **X**

The Story

We carried Boyds Bears in our antiques store (remember, my mom's high school bedroom became our gift room?). This bear was in the store when I arrived to run it in 1993, and my ex-husband (well, he was my husband at the time) had to have it. It reminded him of his childhood bear that he called "Snowy."

Both my kids were given Steiff bears by my grandmother when they were born. Houston's bear never got a name (typical boy) and Indy christened her pink Steiff "Berry." Indy still takes "Berry" with her when we travel.

William sold me a bunch of stuff and I think the bear cost me about $2. I put it on eBay thinking I would be lucky to get $9.99 for it. I immediately received an email from a potential bidder: "The bear looks like the original Binkie. Does she have her hang tag? Thanks!"

I had no idea, so I just said "I don't really know." Even with that answer, the bear ended up selling for a lot of money!

When I decided to include this bear in my book, I started to do some research to find out if it really was "Binkie." I found an expert named Beth Phillips (on eBay—where else?) who writes for *Teddy Bear Review*. What a nice gal! She was more than happy to help me.

Beth's email said:

Lynn, your mystery bear is in fact the elusive gray-nosed Binkie B. Bean. Binkie with the gray nose came out in 1989, style number 5115. The gray nose was only used for a year or two—then he was made with a black nose. There is a third version named Binkie II that is more of a cream color and has gold velveteen paw pads instead of the white felt used on the first Binkie. The Binkie with the gray nose is hard to find and usually sells for a premium. By far the most valuable of the older Boyds are the Himalayan Dancing Bears, the first three Bailey Bears, some of the old Limited Edition dressed sets, the Bubba bears, and a few other hard to find Boyds. Beth

What great information! Here is a little background on Boyds. Boyds' founder, G. M. Lowenthal was born in New York in 1949. After a career in retail with Bloomies, G. M. and his wife, Justina, opened an antiques store in their home (just like my grandma). They soon found that they were doing better selling antique reproductions than true antiques. In 1984 they introduced their first jointed bear. In 1993, they introduced their resin figures. The rest is history.

Snowy, Binkie, and Berry. Amazing what a sentimental item can mean to you as an eBay buyer or seller! At least a $50 profit. And this bear had sat in my grandmother's store for at least two years without finding a buyer. How funny that my grandmother's antiques store (founded in her home) did better than the Lowenthal's antiques store in their home, and we sold Boyds Bears out of my mom's high school bedroom. Crazy!

#39 Bing & Grondahl Parrot

$5.00
Paid
From: Garage sale

Bing & Grondahl Parrot Figurine Vintage Blue Ara 2235 C

Description:
Blue and white and "as-is." 16.5" by 8" by 4.25". This is an amazing figurine in as-is condition. Only around the neck. The rest is in great condition. I was going to send this to a professional repair company for a great repair because these pieces sell for $1,600 when new. The people I bought it from brought it back on the airplane from Denmark and it was damaged in an earthquake. Design by Armand Peterson. A great piece that needs some TLC.

Winning Bid: **$185.50**

Ended: 12/16/06
History: 15 bids
Starting Bid: $9.99
Winner: Glendale, CA

Viewed
000166 X

Bing & Grondahl Parrot   #39

The Story

I love Bing & Grondahl and Royal Copenhagen (as most of you probably already know). So when I saw this as-is piece at a garage sale for $10, I had to admire it, even in its damaged condition. I asked the seller, "This is so sad—what happened?" She told me she and her husband had hand-carried the parrot back from Denmark on the plane, only to have it get damaged later in a Pasadena, CA earthquake. I told her, "That breaks my heart." And I added, "Do you know my friend Hank Maarse whose family owns Jacob Maarse florist?"

"Of course we know of Jacob Maarse." We were on common footing. My friend Hank is the one pictured in the Alfa Romeo in story #36. I said, "I just love this, would you take any less because I will need to pay a lot of money to get it repaired?" She said, "Of course. How about $5?"

I almost kept this piece. Bing & Grondahl and Royal Copenhagen Danish figurines have such an allure for me. My grandmother loved them also and she often hand-carried pieces back from Denmark in her suitcase. She always traveled with an empty suitcase just for that reason! She would take only two travel outfits and inside her first suitcase she would pack that other empty one. Boy, would she freak out today if she knew that the airlines were charging $25 for your first suitcase and sometimes even more for the second!

Bing & Grondahl figurines are famous the world over. The Danish porcelain company has produced over 160 different bird figurines since the 1890s. Wow! This figurine that I sold was more than a parrot,

it was a blue or hyacinth macaw. The hyacinth macaw is the largest macaw and the largest flying parrot in the world. They are native to South America and can grow to be 39" long and 4.4 pounds. Unfortunately, since they are so popular as pets in captivity—selling for $9,000 to $12,000—they are in danger of becoming extinct.

When I researched this figurine, I found that it could sell for $1,600 in perfect condition. With that knowledge, I was very tempted to get the figurine professionally repaired. But then I had to follow my own advice: Never pay for a repair job. Let the new owners decide how much, when, and if they want to pay for it. A repair job can be extremely expensive, and I have found over the years that I do better letting the new owners take care of it. Because no matter how you slice it, a professionally repaired figurine is still an "as is" piece.

"No matter how you slice it" means "No matter how you look at it," and this battered Bing & Grondhal figurine turned my $5 into $185.50—way more than I originally started with!

#40 Majolica Bunny Mug

$2.⁰⁰

Paid

From: Garage sale

Majolica Childrens Mug 1900 Higgins Seiter Bunny Rabbit

Description:
This is a charming French majolica childhood mug. It shows bunny
rabbits eating turnips in a farmer's field. It is embossed with hills
and forests. The handle is a leaping hare (bunny rabbit). Very sweet;
signed and patented by the retailer Higgins and Seiter New York on
December 4th, 1900. There is a crack around the handle and it is
repaired at the base of the handle. 3 tiny chips and crazing as can be
expected with antique majolica. 3.5" by 4.5". Darling.

**Winning
Bid:**

$103.⁵⁰

Ended: 12/18/06
History: 9 bids
Starting Bid: $24.99
Winners: Waynesboro, VA

Viewed

000749 X

Majolica Bunny Mug   #40

The Story

My brother finally talked me into it. It was right before Christmas, and I bought a wireless Sprint card. That $60 per month enabled me to list from anywhere. It was amazing. I could list from Houston's baseball games, from car trips, in an airport, in a restaurant, and I even found the signal to be stronger than my wireless in my own home! What an amazing change in my productivity.

I really got to test it out when we went to Disneyland to celebrate Indy's birthday. In the car ride out, I listed 37 items (and no—I was NOT driving. I can't multitask that well). While checking into the hotel and having lunch, I listed another 22. Eight items were listed during appetizers that evening. During the 45 minutes while I was waiting for the kids to come back from the park after dinner, I listed 24 more items (and no, my kids were not at Disneyland alone—they were with my brother Lee). At lunch the next day and on the ride home, I listed another 45 things. WOW!

Bottom line, I listed 136 items in my down time while on a mini-vacation with my kids. It took 342 minutes, or 5.7 hours—about 2.5 minutes per item, once the initial write-ups were finished on my *I Sell* sheets. Pretty cool.

One of the items that I listed that weekend was this damaged Majolica bunny rabbit child's mug. How cute is it?

I found the mug at a garage sale that had really wonderful items—antique, high quality, but unfortunately priced very high. Then I spotted a stack of eBay and Replacements printouts, which suggested the sellers were hoping to receive Replacements prices for their goods, and I was ready to leave. Instead, I took a deep breath and asked myself, "What would Cheryl Leaf do?"

Cheryl Leaf would offer to buy the entire garage full and ask the seller to name a price. I did just that. The seller hemmed and hawed and invited me to make an offer. I told her that it looked like she had already researched everything and knew its value. I did not.

I waited, and she finally said "$400." I took a few minutes to have another look around. I would have gone to $500, but she didn't need to know that. And I couldn't accept too quickly or she would think her price was too low—but I did accept.

So I got 200 items at $2 per piece. This rabbit mug was a serious winner. The signature "Higgins & Seiter" meant it had been sold at the Higgins & Seiter retail store on 22nd Street in New York City, which opened in 1887.

Higgins & Seiter had a full-time commissions agent in Paris to locate the best goods for the store, which was famous in every part of the US for its enormous stock of "choice" goods—rich cut glass, fine china, art pottery, wedding presents, and so on. The funny part of this story is that my grandma (Cheryl Leaf) was from the Higgins & Seiter generation. She loved the word "choice," and interestingly enough, she loved Disneyland. I miss my grandma.

#41 Avocado Head

50¢

Paid

From: Garage sale

Mexico Handpainted Avacado Head Weird Bizzare Creepy

Description:

This unusual piece is signed "Mexico." Hand-painted avocado is in the shape of a head. Weird and slightly bizarre. Face is haunting and creepy. 6" by 3½". Vintage. Needs cleaning. Pottery.

Winning Bid:

$12.⁹⁹

Ended: 12/18/06
History: 1 bid (sold in store)
Starting Bid: $12.99
Winner: Maryland

Viewed

000048 X

Avocado Head #41

The Story

Can you believe I misspelled "avocado" in my auction title (ha ha!)? And I am just realizing that I spelled "bizarre" and "hand-painted" incorrectly also. Apparently that didn't matter so much, because I spelled "weird" correctly.

Here is an email that I got from the buyer:

Hi Lynn, The reason I bought the avocado head is because every Christmas my childhood friend and I try to outdo each other in finding the weirdest possible gifts for each other. It has become a tradition that now our kids look forward to because of the shock factor. The tradition started years ago before eBay existed. Once eBay came along, I was able to simply search for items with keywords like bizarre, weird, strange, scary, WTF, creepy, unearthly, awful etc. These searches have provided me with some unbelievably strange stuff that most people would be disgusted by. "Avocado Head" fit the bill pretty well since the face is quite strange at certain angles. Good Luck, thanks, Nick

I had to laugh when I got Nick's email. I was writing this story and didn't want to offend the buyer by saying how strange this item was. Whew!

My family had a Christmas tradition that was very similar. We kept regifting one scary doll and one scary doll head.

When I was in Bellingham over the summer, I went out to dinner with my Boot Campers and my high school friend Marlene Thurston. Marlene commented, "You have some really creepy stuff on eBay. What is the story behind that avocado head?" Her asking about it probably made it sell.

Why would someone in Mexico make an avocado with a face? Well, as I researched avocados I found that they have quite a long and rich history. The avocado is a revered vegetable. Oops. An avocado is a fruit, and not a vegetable. It is part of the berry family. It also provides very healthy fat and my nutritionist is always urging me to eat more avocados.

The word "avocado" comes from the Hahuatl word *āhuacatl* which means "testicle." Avocados were known by the Aztecs as a fertility fruit. Apparently, if you wanted to appear chaste (pure and innocent) in ancient times, you did not eat them. How funny.

Avocados are grown mostly in warm regions like South and Central America. They are a very profitable crop and many come out of Mexico. It is no wonder, then, that the Mexican artists would have made a figural avocado to sell. I *do* wonder, though, why they painted such a creepy face on it. Oh, well, Nick's family got a kick out of this one that Christmas! And I got a kick out of our green doll head on a different Christmas!

#42 Furio Christmas Plates

$2.⁰⁰/2

Paid

From: Garage sale

Boxed Set 4 Christmas Salad Plates Furio Fir Tree NICE

Description:
Hand-painted boxed set of Christmas salad plates from Furio. White, red and green. Christmas pattern. Boxed set of 4. 7½". Look to be in new, unused condition. We have another boxed set up for sale in a separate auction.

Winning Bid:

$47.⁹⁹/2

Ended: 12/24/06
History: 20 bids/2
Starting Bid: $9.99 ea
Winner: IL, VT

Viewed
 X

Furio Christmas Plates   #42

The Story

I picked these dishes up for $1 a box at a garage sale. Furio sounded familiar to me but I wasn't quite sure why. The plates were cute and still in the original boxes. I thought it was worth a shot. I listed them on eBay the week before Christmas. I guess my timing was pretty good, because they sold for way more than I would have ever imagined. One set sold for $26 and the other for $21.99.

During one of our Queen's Court calls, Jarsie emailed me to tell me that Furio was a Target brand. You have got to be kidding me! I think these plates sold for more than they would have cost originally at Target. I love Target. It is one of my favorite stores.

I started digging for information on Target and here is what I found. In 1902, George D. Dayton opened a retail store called "Goodfellows" in downtown Minneapolis, Minnesota. That is why Target headquarters are still located there. In 1946, The Dayton Company decided to revise its bylaws to ensure that it would always give 5% of pre-tax profits back to the community. How cool is that?

In 1962, Dayton entered the discount store market with the opening of the first Target store. Its mission was to offer popular national brands at discounted prices. The wide-open aisles made a fun shopping experience. They also implemented "plan-o-grams" so that each and every Target store, no matter where, followed the same blueprint, with similar items found in the same location. It sounds kind of like the "plan-o-gram" we use in my eBay room—104 shelves labeled from "A" to "ZZZZ" so that we can always (hopefully) locate our items when they sell!

In 1969, Dayton merged with the Hudson retail chain, creating Dayton-Hudson. What I found really amazing is that in 1985, the Target advertising circular was second only to the Sunday comics as America's most read newspaper insert. In 2000, Dayton-Hudson was renamed the Target Corporation. The company now has over 1,300 stores.

I emailed the Target Company to ask more about their Furio brand. Here is the response I received:

> Good afternoon Lynn -
> Thank you for your inquiry. I would like to clarify that Furio is not a Target owned brand.
> Thanks, Michaela

However, in a 1993 article in *Discount Store News,* I found this: "'Target has its own trend merchandising group that travels the world in search of the next hit products,' Target spokesman Macke said, singling out Mediterranean-inspired dinnerware sold under Target's Furio private label."

All I can figure out is that Furio (made in Italy) was at one point a Target label, but is not any longer. So don't overlook Furio or another popular Target brand, "Home." I have done very well with these brands. And why not? Target has been around for 46 years and built up a very loyal following. I am sure many homes use the Furio and Home brands in their dining rooms. Let's help them find additional pieces with our eBay auctions!

#43 Cherub Tray

$2.00 Paid
From: Garage sale

Antique Victorian Cherub Angel Silverplate Art Nouveau

Description:
This tray is silver plated and has a handle. 11" by 8" by 1½". Angels or cherubs. Darling. Signed with "EPNS" only. There is some silver polish residue which may clean up. Some wear to the silver plate but still an amazing piece. I would guess 1890s to 1930s.

Winning Bid: **$104.⁴⁹**

Ended: 12/26/06
History: 10 bids
Starting Bid: $9.99
Winners: Australia

Viewed
 X

The Story

I thought this belonged to my grandmother, but then I realized that I had bought this darling tray at a sale for $2. It was only signed with "EPNS," which stands for "Electro Plated Nickel Silver," a generic term found on a lot of silver plated hollowware items. Hollowware is what the metal serving pieces on a train's dining car were called. They complemented the china and today the term "hollowware" is still used for things like metal sugar bowls, pitchers, teapots and trays.

This tray sold on the day President Ford passed away. Gerald R. Ford was born as Leslie Lynch King, Jr. His mother, Dorothy, separated from his father just sixteen days later on July 30, 1913. After several years, she married Gerald Rudolff Ford, and at the age of three, Leslie King became Gerald R. Ford, Jr.. He was raised in Grand Rapids, Michigan.

President and Betty Ford were long-time residents of our valley. They had lived in Rancho Mirage for over 30 years. He was very well-liked and respected in our community.

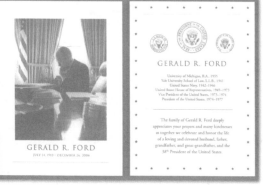

GERALD R. FORD
JULY 14, 1913 - DECEMBER 26, 2006

GERALD R. FORD

University of Michigan, B.A. 1935
Yale University School of Law, L.L.B., 1941
United States Navy, 1942-1946
United States House of Representatives, 1949-1973
Vice President of the United States, 1973-1974
President of the United States, 1974-1977

The family of Gerald R. Ford deeply
appreciates your prayers and many kindnesses
as together we celebrate and honor the life
of a loving and devoted husband, father,
grandfather, and great-grandfather, and the
38th President of the United States.

Ford's family decided to have a public viewing of his casket at their church in Palm Desert. It was scheduled to start on Friday night at 4 pm and would end on Saturday morning at 8 am. My mom and I decided that we just had to go pay our respect, but to avoid crowds we would go in the middle of the night. I mean, how often does a former president pass away in your city? They had closed some roads in anticipation of huge crowds, and the only way to get to the church was to park some distance away and take a shuttle bus.

I told my brother what we were doing and he said to me, "Are you doing this so that you will have things to write about in your ezine and books?" No! Life is just more fun when you mix it up.

I woke up at 2 am, called my mom, and off we went. We arrived to find the shuttle stop looking like a ghost town, so we were able to get on a bus immediately. We were not allowed to take our purses, cameras, or cell phones with us.

It was a very surreal experience to see President Ford's casket with the American flag draped over it and the honor guards standing so still they looked like statues watching over him. We were given a memorial card from the family.

Paying our respect was worth getting up in the middle of the night, and it made me realize how important all of my friends and family are to me. I was also thrilled that the cherub tray that sold for over $100 hadn't belonged to my grandmother. It made it so much easier to part with!

#44 Z & S Rose Plate

$1.⁰⁰
Paid
From: Garage sale

Antique Serving Cake Plate 2 Handles Rose ZS Co Bavaria

Description:
10.5" by 9.5" roses. White, gold, green and pink are the colors.
Lovely plate in very good condition for its age with some slight hair-
line cracks. It is signed "ZS & Co Bavaria" in green. I would guess
1890s.

**Winning
Bid:**

$51.⁹⁸

Ended: 1/1/07
History: 19 bids
Starting Bid: $9.99
Winner: West Virginia

Viewed
 **X**

Z & S Rose Plate   #44

The Story

I got this beautiful antique plate with hand-painted roses on it for $1 at a garage sale. It was signed with "ZS Co." The "ZS" stood for Zeh, Scherzer & Co that was founded in 1880. This German company was well known for making a wide range of china, including coffee and tea sets, tableware, and decorative porcelain.

This plate was definitely a piece of decorative porcelain. I decided that I would call this a two-handled cake plate. Most of us know what a pedestal cake stand looks like, but may not recognize this as a cake plate.

Because of its commercial success, Zeh, Scherzer & Co opened its own art department in 1908 and hired Professor Fritz Klee as an advisor. What a unique and interesting personality Professor Fritz Klee was. You just have to love the name. It reminds me of Professor Caractacus Potts from *Chitty Chitty Bang Bang*—one of my favorite movies ever!

But back to Fritz Klee: he was born in 1876 and died in 1976, living to be over 100 years old. How cool is that? He is considered a pioneer of modern porcelain production. He was an architect and designer and worked for many famous companies. Anything signed with his name can sell for big bucks on eBay. It's now a goal of mine to find one of his personal pieces. He retired in 1939 at the age of 63, but lived another 37 years. The idea of living for that long without working was one reason that my grandmother never retired—she felt that doing work you loved was the best way to keep your mind agile.

The products made by Zeh & Scherzer during that time period were spectacular and are extremely collectible: Art Deco items, as well as figurines of people, animals and fantasy figures. Collectors rate the years from 1908 to 1919 as the company's greatest period.

Z & S continued to grow and develop a reputation for high quality goods. By about 1985, the company changed its name to simply "Scherzer & Co." or even just "Sherzer 1880," but began to struggle as cheap goods from Asia started to flood the market.

In 1991, the company was taken over by an investment company which immediately reduced production. In 1992, all production was halted. Too sad.

My grandmother loved roses, and would often drive up Illinois Street to admire the Cornwall Rose Garden. That is why I always buy European items with roses on them. My grandma loved Europe and she loved roses. I couldn't go wrong with this piece.

What is really ironic is that this plate sold on the very day that my team, the USC Trojans, beat Michigan in the "Rose" Bowl. It was a great day in Pasadena for USC fans.

My mom, Houston and I attended the game and had a wonderful time, while my brother Lee took Indy to the American Girl Doll Revue, since she doesn't really love football. In fact, she may be allergic to it. Just kidding!

Then we stayed overnight at the Ritz Carlton in Pasadena and celebrated my awesome brother's birthday the next day poolside. It was a blast, and I made over $50 on this special Rose Bowl plate!

#45 Gypsy Cloth Doll

$2.00
Paid
From: Garage sale

Gypsy Belly Dancer Toy Works Doll Cloth Silk Lady Rare

Description:
Neat vintage doll. Tag on the side says, "The Toy Works Inc. Middle Falls, NY made in USA." Looks old. This appears to be a gypsy or belly dancer. Very large. 32" by 14" by 4". Caricature. I think it feels like silk but don't know for sure and it needs cleaning. Some wear.

Winning Bid:

$51.00
Ended: 1/6/07
History: 7 bids
Starting Bid: $9.99
Winner: Tucson, AZ

Viewed
 **X**

Gypsy Cloth Doll #45

The Story

I am sitting at dinner with Indiana as I write this story. She is doing her homework and I have my laptop out. Our waitress, Lauren, thinks the entire thing is pretty cute as mom and daughter do their work together. The reason we are at dinner is because Houston has a baseball scrimmage across the street in 45 minutes and we needed to eat.

I had just mentioned to Indy this morning how much easier it is to write books since the advent of the Internet (which Al Gore invented, by the way—just kidding). Before the Internet and Google, I had to actually go into a library and do my research. How could you ever write a book in a few months? It could take years!

I had so much fun Googling "The Toy Works" earlier today, and the information I found was fascinating. Also, because it is still in business, I could email a photo of this doll and ask for help identifying it. Amazing!

So, while we were sitting there, Indy said, "I have to analyze this poem by Emily Dickinson. What expression is like 'hurried slow' in these multiple choice answers?" I said, "Let me Google that." I couldn't find one darn thing. By the way, I have never been asked to analyze an Emily Dickinson poem and I have a Master's Degree. Indy is only in fourth grade. What is the world coming to? Indy's dad suggested 'sweet sorrow,' which uses opposite meanings to make a point, like 'hurried slow' does.

Luckily with eBay, you learn new things every day. In my fun Google investigation I found that "The Toy Works" is now known as "Fiddler's Elbow," and it has been in business for 36 years. I have to say that I thought this doll was much older than 36 years. Just goes to show you that you can't get everything right.

In 1973, the company's founder, John Gunther, visited the Museum of the City of New York and saw an exhibition of nineteenth-century cloth toys. These toys were intricately printed using antique hand-engraved copper rollers. This exhibition inspired Gunther to start his "Toy Works" company, reproducing these amazing rag toys from the 1890s using modern silk-screening techniques. The company is located in the foothills of the Adirondack Mountains in New York and is still in business. Too cool!

In 2001, "The Toy Works" lines were discontinued and the "Fiddler's Elbow" named emerged. The company product line shifted from cloth rag toys to gifts and home décor. They now license many famous artists, including Mary Engelbreit.

No wonder I thought my doll was older. It was a reproduction of those wonderful 1890s rag dolls. Since the line has been discontinued, I think any "Toy Works" doll in good condition is worth picking up. My gypsy sold for over $50 and I must admit I was shocked. But now, thanks to the Internet and Google (my friend) we know why. Expensive cheap!

#46 French Chop Plates

$25.⁰⁰/8

Paid

From: Estate sale

French Longchamp Nemour Chop Plates

Description:
French large platter. 12½" and this is much larger than the 11½" chop plate that the company also made. We have quite a few of these large round serving platters chop plates up for sale this week in separate auctions. You are bidding on one. The pattern is "Nemours" by Longchamp. Made in France. Multicolor flowers floral pattern. Blue ring and cream body. Discontinued around 1973. A lovely pattern. I did my research and people call it majolica, but I think it is more faience in style. No chips, no cracks, no crazing.

Winning Bid: $171.⁹³/8

Ended: 1/28/07
History: 10 bids/8
Starting Bid: $9.99, $24.99
Winner: KY, MI, TX

Viewed

000665 X

French Chop Plates   #46

The Story

I bought a pile of these huge chop plates at an estate sale for $25. There were eight of them, two of which had minor damage. They were the largest chop plate made and no price was listed for them on Replacements. The dinner plates, however, listed for $109.95. Wow!

In retrospect, I probably should have started the bidding at $49.99 each for the good ones and $24.99 each for the damaged ones. Instead, I wanted to move them and thought the lower starting bid price would cause a bidding frenzy. I started the good ones at $24.99 and the damaged ones at $9.99. If there isn't a lot of demand for an item, starting at a lower price doesn't work to get people bidding against each other. The plates didn't go much higher than their opening bids, but I still made almost $150 on the transaction.

Let me explain what a chop plate is. It is typically an inch or two larger (at about 13") than a dinner plate, and is also known as a "round serving platter." It was originally made to serve meats, and that is probably where the "chop" comes from. "Chop" means "to cut into pieces"; it also refers to a certain cut of meat. A meat chop is cut perpendicularly to the spine, usually contains a rib, and is served as an individual portion—think lamb or pork chop.

When I went to research the Longchamp company that made these wonderful French plates, I hit a wall. The only Longchamp company I could find is the famous leather and luxury goods company founded in 1948 by Jean Cassegrain. The company was named for the famous Longchamp horse race track in Paris, which translates to "Long Field." That is why it uses a horse as its logo.

The company began by creating leather coverings for pipes and other products for smokers. By 1955, it had expanded to small leather goods. By 1980, it added clothing and other fashion accessories. Nowhere could I find that Longchamp made dinnerware, but I assumed that at some point they must have.

I was wrong! Longchamp's NY PR firm emailed to let me know that they weren't made by Longchamp. The manufacturer is still a mystery.

The reason I called these plates "faience" instead of "majolica" is because "faience" is French tin glazed wear that is similar to Delft ware and majolica. These plates were French, so "faience" was the best term.

As these were listed and being bid upon, I had the opportunity to take Houston and my mom to a luncheon where Pete Carroll (USC football coach) was the keynote speaker. Houston is a huge fan, so I let him miss school and bought the $50-per-person tickets. Hey, the profit on these plates paid for that! Pretty cool. Pete Carroll is the nicest man; he spent some time talking to Houston, autographed a football for him, and posed for pictures. It was a really neat experience—and all financed by my mysterious Longchamp chop plates!

#47 Majolica Hen Basket

$12.00
Paid
From: Estate sale

Este Italy Majolica Nesting Hen Basket Vintage RARE

Description:
Awesome piece is signed "Este Made in Italy." This is being sold as is, which is very typical with antique majolica. The base has 8 to 12 tiny rough spots. The top looks to be in excellent condition with one tiny spot on the hen's beak. Both handles of the basket are repaired at each side and at the top. I would guess 1920s to 1950s and a very hard-to-find piece in majolica. Eggs are on the hen's nest. Greenish yellow, grey, black, brown, orange and white. I bought a lot of great items recently from a very expensive estate.

Winning Bid: **$209.49**

Ended: 2/2/07
History: 25 bids
Starting Bid: $49.99, $24.99
Winner: North Carolina

Viewed
 000128 X

Majolica Hen Basket   #47

The Story

This piece is called a hen-on-nest covered dish. "HON" is the acronym for hen-on-nest, and HON items are super collectible. My grandma had always just called them "nesting hens," but now I know the proper terminology, I realize I should have used "Hen on Nest" in the title.

The funny thing is that the first time I listed this item, I started the bidding at $49.99 and got NO bids. I relisted it at $24.99, and even with the wrong wording in the title, it sold for over $200! What a great argument for my theory that the lower you start an auction, the greater the odds that it will go high. (My theory didn't work for those chop plates, though.)

Anyway, I had been in Scottsdale for the weekend. When I returned on Sunday afternoon, I knew that I needed to find some stock to sell on eBay! My friend Ben was having an estate sale and he invited me to stop by at around 3 pm when it was ending. I walked in and couldn't believe how much was left.

The house was chug-a-rum full (as my grandmother would say), meaning that the rooms were filled from floor to ceiling.

The items left in this estate sale were incredible and reminded me of the things my grandmother carried in her antiques store. Fenton, cranberry, majolica, a shoe and chair collection—and most items were made in Europe. Ben said he would sell me all that was left at 30% of the marked prices. I bought it all for $3,200.

The problem was how to pack it all up and get it moved into my garage.

Absolutely no way this was going to fit into my house! I had received an email earlier in the week from Sharla Jackson, one of my Live Boot Camp double grads, saying that she was going to be in Palm Springs for her birthday. I called her and asked her if I could hire her to help me pack it up. She said it would be a blast to just experience the sale and that I didn't have to pay her.

What a sweetie (or should I say HON?)! Well, my mom, Sharla, and I got everything packed up in about two and a half hours. It took two loads in my mom's minivan and one load in my BMW to get it moved to my house. I was just starting to clear a place in my garage for my car (now that the darn Alfa was gone) but alas, it was not to be. Where my car should have been parked was now a pile of eBay loot. And I have to admit that even two years later, I still haven't listed all that great stuff. Shame on me!

But back to the covered hen (oops, I mean "HON"). It was marked at $40, so it cost me $12. There are entire collectors' books written about hens or roosters on nests; it is a very lucrative area, and well worth knowing more about.

This particular HON was signed with "Este" and "Made in Italy." Este is a town in northern Italy that is very well known for farming, industry and crafts. This hen was one of those famous crafts, and even with all the damage, the nicks and the handle repairs, she still brought me an almost $200 profit! I wonder what other goodies are still sitting outside in my chug-a-rum full garage?

#48 Farm Animal Plates

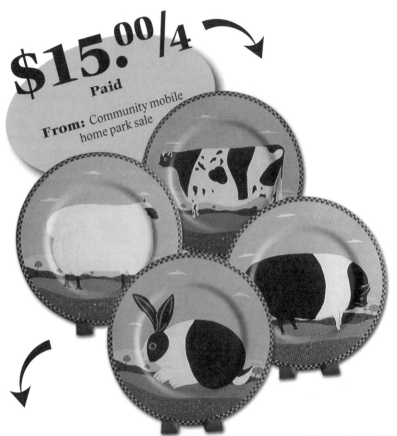

$15.00/4
Paid

From: Community mobile home park sale

Warren Kimble Hand Painted Big Bunny Rabbit Plate NEAT

Description:
Black and cream. We have four of these plates listed this week in separate auctions. This plate was designed exclusively by Warren Kimble for Cape Craftsmen, Inc. Hand painted and super heavy. Mostly green with a checkerboard band. Very French country folk art. 8½". Excellent condition.

Winning Bid: **$137.51/4**

Ended: 2/8/07
History: 13 bids/4
Starting Bid: $9.99 ea auction
Winners: Sparta, NJ

Viewed

000198 X

Farm Animal Plates #48

The Story

It was the weekend before my vacation on the Cayman Islands with Peter. There were only ten garage sales for the entire valley, and my mom I planned to hit most of them.

Houston had a basketball (yes, basketball!) game at 10 am in Indio and I told him I would not be able to make it. He became very upset and wouldn't look at me or answer me. I told him, "If it is that important to you, talk to me and I will make an effort."

Instead, he looked so sad. He has a hard time expressing his feelings, just like I do. Finally, he said "Mommy, you are going to be gone for a week. I want you to be there."

What do you say to that? Of course I was going to be there. My mom and I changed our route, skipping several of the sales we had planned to hit, and adding a community garage sale in Indio that started at 7 am and went until noon. We normally don't include Indio in our route, but because of Houston we decided to head over to that one after the game.

After the last buzzer at 11:30, we raced over to the Indio community sale. Oh, my gosh—we should have been there at 7 am. There were 50 tables of items, a hot dog cart and people already packing up. Bummer!

Whenever there is a concession stand or hot dog cart at a community sale, you know you have hit the jackpot! It's a sign that you're going to find something great. I'm not kidding. This is serious insider information.

Another thing that I have learned from years of doing this is that what is meant to be yours is meant to be yours. I don't pound on people's doors at 5 am, and I don't run people over to get to items. I take it slow and steady. Slow and steady often wins the race. Think about the tortoise and the hare.

In one of the booths that hadn't yet been taken down, I found four plates made by Warren Kimble. I had never heard of Kimble before, but the seller clearly thought there was a market for his work—she had the plates priced at $10 each. Since it was the end of the sale, she sold me all four for $15.

You see, these plates were meant to be mine. They had gone through five hours of a sale and had been passed over by everyone. My point is this—no matter what time it is during the sale, there will always be something worth buying. It goes back to what my grandmother taught me: "There is a sleeper in every store."

Warren Kimble is a very interesting man and artist. Born in New Jersey and educated at Syracuse University, painting was always his passion. His art is whimsical and appeals to the child and art lover in all of us—or a lot of us, at any rate. In 2006, his licensing contracts were estimated at over $100 million annually. Now that is some rabbit feed!

The plates I bought portrayed four different farm animals: a pig, a cow, a sheep and a rabbit. They all sold to the same lady for over $130 and were shipped to New Jersey. The plate that sold for the most—$100.23—was a bunny rabbit. Why else would I make so many rabbit inferences during this story? Sometimes the hare does win the race—but then again, there was no tortoise in this competition.

#49 Beaded Fireplace Screen

$2.⁰⁰
Paid
From: Garage sale

Antique Beaded Fireplace Screen Cover Angels Beads WOW

Description:
Beaded cut-out portion from a fireplace screen (I think). 14" by 13".
Angels or cupids or cherub. Amazing. Burgundy red with grey, black
and white. This is an amazing piece. In good condition. Edges are
unraveling. I would guess 1890s or so. Victorian era. Needs some
work. Would look amazing in a frame or as a pillow.

Winning Bid: **$132.⁴⁷**

Ended: 2/9/07
History: 9 bids
Starting Bid: $24.99
Winner: Carpentersville, IL

Viewed

000202 X

Beaded Fireplace Screen #49

The Story

I was in the Cayman Islands on vacation as this awesome piece was selling. Peter decided to do an extra scuba dive and I sat on our balcony overlooking the pool and ocean and started writing my third *100 Best* book—*Kaching!* I love the Cayman Islands. We took great scuba trips, saw the turtle farm, drove to the far side of the island, and just enjoyed the atmosphere and restaurants.

We were also there during Super Bowl Sunday. There were so many Americans visiting that the Westin Las Casuarina Resort put up a huge screen TV in the lounge. We watched the cold game in front of the fireplace as the warm trade winds passed by the huge ocean view windows. Unfortunately, the Chicago Bears lost, but it was still a blast.

Speaking of fireplaces, I had found this antique beaded piece at a garage sale and couldn't figure out what it was. I stared at it for quite some time, and then I remembered that on my grandmother's mantle, she had something similar. It was square and on a frame; she told me that in Victorian times, they would put these elaborate beaded pieces in front of the fireplaces to make them more attractive.

These screens also had a utilitarian purpose: they were used to control where the heat from the fire would be directed. They were put on a stand that rotated. Wow! That was long before central heat!

Fireplaces really became popular during the Victorian era. In addition to providing heat (I personally hate being cold!), people also started to view fire-places as a

part of the décor that could add charm to a room. As housing styles changed, so did the appearance of the typical fireplace: think gaudy, ornate, simple, mission style, Batchelder tiles, Victorian, Eames era sleek, and so on.

Although the appearance of the fireplace has varied radically over time, basic fireplace technology remains constant. It consists of two elements: the surround and the insert.

The surround is the mantle and sides and is typically made of wood, marble, iron, or granite. The insert is the part of the fireplace where the fire burns. This insert is always cast iron.

What I found incredibly interesting is that Benjamin Franklin played a role in the invention of a type of fireplace. He realized that fireplaces lose an enormous amount of heat through the wall into which they are built. To prevent this loss, he created the first free-standing fireplace designed to sit in the middle of the room. Brilliant Ben! This became known as the "Franklin stove." Even I have heard of that!

Speaking of brilliant... well, I would never call myself "brilliant," but I have to give myself a little bit of credit for buying this fireplace beaded screen for only $2 and having it sell for over $130. And for also being smart enough to watch the freezing cold 2007 Super bowl on Grand Cayman in front of a fireplace—a fireplace that (by the way) did NOT need to be turned on!

#50 Replique Perfume Bottle

$20.⁰⁰

Paid

From: Garage sale

Replique Perfume Display Bottle Raphael Paris Tulip WOW

Description:
This is such an amazing piece. It is 3.5" by 4.75" by 9.25" tall. Very cracked and "as is" but does hold green water. Stopper is in the shape of a tulip. There is a gold cord with a wax seal. The wax seal is red and has an "R" on it. Cool vintage store display piece. Says "Replique Perfume Raphael Paris."

Winning Bid:

$82.⁸¹

Ended: 2/26/07
History: 5 bids
Starting Bid: $24.99
Winner: Germany

Viewed

000106 X

Replique Perfume Bottle #50

The Story

I found this at a garage sale here in the desert. As we walked in, I looked at my mom and said, "This is the same house where that really nice lady asked $1 for the Pucci-style dress that you sold for over $100."

Once we were inside, it seemed to me and my mom that everything was a little pricey. This perfume bottle was ticketed at $35. I asked the seller if she remembered me and my mom, and she said she did. I also asked her if she would take any less for this because it was so damaged. She agreed to $20.

I liked it because it was quite large and was most likely a store display piece. Any type of store display piece seems to sell for quite a bit, and perfume bottles are the best. Perfume bottle collectors are an awesome bunch.

Replique (the perfume I bought) was made in the 1940s by Raphael in Paris, France. My research suggested that this bottle was made between 1944 and 1947—right after the end of World War II—and described the perfume as a "refined, mossy, woody fragrance." It was originally recommended for evening wear. Can you even imagine having one perfume for day and one for evening? I wear Clinique "Happy" all day, every day because it makes me happy!

The practice of wearing perfume is thousands of years old. The English word "perfume" comes from the Latin *"per fumus"* which means "through smoke," because the original "perfumes" were the burning incenses and herbs used in religious services. The Egyptians were the first to introduce perfume into the mainstream by rubbing perfumed oils and ointments on their bodies, and many other cultures followed. Over the centuries, the bottles that hold perfumes have become seriously collectible. Incredible!

While I was researching perfume bottles, I came across an article by Michele Alice for AuctionBytes. AuctionBytes.com is an amazing free news source for online merchants. I really respect the founder and editor, Ina Steiner—she is awesome! I even have a photo with her.

According to Michele's article, most perfume bottle collectors can't afford (or don't have space for) all of the different categories of bottles, so they specialize. They might select a particular type of bottle (figurals, atomizers), a maker (Wedgwood, Lalique), a country of origin (Czech, French), an era (Art Deco, Art Nouveau), one specific size (mini, store display), a single color, a perfume company, or an actual fragrance.

Next they look for condition. Is the bottle "MIP" (mint in package)? Does it have the original hang tags or tokens (luckily, mine did)? Michele advises collectors always to buy the best, most complete specimen that they can afford. Interesting. My grandma used to give the same advice. Love that.

The next factor to consider is rarity. Very old, pre-nineteenth century hand-made signed pieces are an incredible investment. And finally, aesthetic merit comes into play. What is beautiful and what is not? I'll tell you what is beautiful. My $20 investment turning into $82.81 in seven days!

#51 Sterling Nut Dishes

$1.00 Paid
From: Garage sale

Sterling 104 Iris Nut Master Dish Gorham Art Nouveau ?

Description:
We have 5 pieces in this pattern up for sale in separate auctions. It is an amazing pattern and I think rare and antique. Any help with identifying it would be appreciated. Signed with "104 Gorham Sterling" and what looks like a script "D." This master (larger) piece is 4" by 8". Some pitting. I don't know if this will clean up. Very Art Nouveau. Looks like an iris or lily; lily leaves, buds, and a handle at one end. Wonderful 1900s to 1920s I would guess.

Winning Bid: $218.⁶²/5

Ended: 2/27/07
History: 34 bids/5
Starting Bid: $9.99 ea auction
Winner: FL, OH, CA

Viewed
 X

Sterling Nut Dishes #51

The Story

My mom and I were out garage saling and decided to venture into Indio. As you have read in this book, we rarely do that, but for some reason one of the sales sounded amazing. But, as luck would have it, we had a LOT of trouble finding it. Even with our Thomas Guide, we just kept driving around and around.

My mom wanted to give up, but I wouldn't let her—and I am so glad we didn't. As we finally pulled into the correct cul-de-sac, we saw all sorts of antiques laid out on the ground. I picked up this tiny set of silver dishes and asked how much. $1 for five dishes. My eyes are so bad it was a miracle that I could even make out the "sterling" written on the base—but I did! I figured that they were nut dishes. My grandmother loved all types of nuts.

Gorham is a very famous American silver company that was founded in Providence, Rhode Island by Jabez Gorham (a master craftsman) and Henry Webster. They started out primarily making coin silver spoons. "Coin silver" spoons were 90% silver and 10% copper (as opposed to the 92.5% silver required for sterling). It gets its name because the 90/10 ratio was the legal minimum required for producing coins.

In 1842, a tariff was put in place that blocked importing silverware from outside the US. This certainly helped Gorham (and all American silver companies). During the heyday of American silver manufacturing (1850 to 1940), Gorham was very influential.

One reason that Gorham was so successful was that it would come out with different flatware patterns every year. This was in direct opposition to English companies in the 1880s, who only offered two styles: "Fiddle" or "Old English"! Not only did Gorham create new patterns each year, but they produced some popular patterns year after year. These included "Lily," "Beaded," "King's Pattern," and "Queen's Pattern." The Queen's Pattern would have been my favorite!

The White house has used many Gorham patterns. Mary Todd Lincoln chose a Gorham tea service, and George W. Bush picked "Chantilly" for Air Force One. In 1967, Gorham was purchased by a company called Textron. Many people felt that Textron moved the company away from its tradition of quality—but its ownership didn't last too long. In 1991, Gorham was sold again, to a company called Brown-Forma, and in 2005 it was sold to Department 56. How strange that they are now owned by Dept. 56? We all know what that is!

I think my pieces were probably 1920s. I never did identify the pattern, but that apparently didn't matter. Can you believe that these dishes sold for over $200 on a $1 investment? A master nut dish would hold all the nuts that were being served and then the smaller individual dishes would be passed out to family members to serve themselves. And according to family consensus, my grandmother's would have held peanuts or almonds!

#52 USC Clothing

$960.00
Paid
From: Closeout

XL USC Nike NWT Wool Fleece Lettermans Jacket $200 WOW

Description:
Great jacket is USC Nike. The body is 75% wool, 20% nylon and 5% other. Lining is nylon. Fill is polyester. Knit band at collar, sleeve and hem. Snap-front closure. Quilted lining with inside zippered pocket. Outer two slash pockets. Left front has "Trojans" and logo and back says "USC." Retail on tag is $200. Nike authentic team apparel. Size XL. I bought a lot of new USC Nike items with tags. There may be slight marks from storage, but I guarantee them all to be official and brand new.

Eventual Total: **$4,859.55**

Ended: 2/27/07 and beyond
History: 94 bids/16 (auction only pcs)
Starting Bid: $9.99 ea auction
Winner: CT, MN, CA, ID, PA, FL, NY

Viewed
001160 X

USC Clothing #52

The Story

Every once in a while you stumble across a great buying opportunity, as I did in 2007. I found a huge quantity of closeout USC Nike XL apparel—192 pieces for $960. It was like Christmas in February! New with tags is always good, XL is great, Nike is even better, and USC authorized merchandise is best of all. Amazing!

My mom and I had a field day going through it all. We let Houston pick out what he wanted and I put his selections away for future gifts. Then we inventoried it all and found that there were sixteen different styles in varying quantities. I decided to test it all at auction before listing it in my store, starting each auction at $9.99. Once I knew what an item sold for at auction, I would double the price and list the remaining items in my eBay store.

You all know that I am a huge USC fan, since I went there twice! The first time was for my undergraduate degree, Entrepreneurship. The second time was for my master's in finance and marketing. It is funny (and I rarely admit this to anyone), but I did apply to the Anderson School of Business at UCLA for my master's. Yikes! Should I really put that in writing? But the bottom line is this, I didn't get accepted to Anderson (stupid UCLA!), and USC gave me a TA (Teacher's Assistant) job that paid for half of my tuition. Tuition then was $7,500 per semester.

Let's look at USC's history. USC (The University of Southern California) was founded in the fall of 1880 when the population of LA was only 11,000. Wow! The University started with 53 students and a faculty of ten. It originated as a private co-educational university under the sponsorship of the Methodist Conference of Southern California, but is currently non-denominational. It still occupies its original site three miles south of downtown LA.

When the school opened in 1880, tuition was $15 per term. That is 500 times less than what I paid for graduate school! Also, students were not allowed to leave town without the knowledge and consent of the university president. I don't think James Zumberge (the president during my years there) even knew my name! When USC was founded, LA didn't have paved streets, electric lights, telephones or a fire system.

What a long way we have come! The USC students are now called the "Trojans" because in 1912, an LA Times sports writer marveled that the football team "fought on like the Trojans." The USC football team (established in 1888) is a football powerhouse with eleven national championships. They have won more NCAA men's individual and team titles than any other university. Fight on!

I am so proud to be a Trojan. And because of USC's rich history, these items I purchased eventually made me $3,899 after about a year. That would have paid for half of one semester's tuition when I was getting my master's. Start saving for your kids' college educations now!

#53 Lucite Box Purses

$50.⁰⁰/2
Paid
From: Estate sale

Lucite Box Purse Eames 1950s Bakelite Handmade Copper
Lucite Box Purse Eames 1950s Bakelite Florida Handbags

Description:

Neat box purse. 6" by 8.25" by 2 5/8" wide. Handmade in British Hong Kong. Pearlized copper and gold swirls. In very good condition with minor scratches. Box style with hinged top. Lined in peach faille. Very clean. NEAT!

Lucite Handbag has a clear acrylic lid and handle in a diamond pattern. Clever ball clasp in Brass. Made by Florida Handbags Made in Miami. Dirty and underside is foggy. 5" by 7". Darling purse.

Winning Bid: **$183.³⁰/2**

Ended: 3/3/07
History: 22 bids/2
Starting Bid: $24.99 ea
Winner: Austria, Belgium

Viewed
000723 X

Lucite Box Purses   #53

The Story

As I was writing this story and typing in my description, I realized that there is no way that I wrote these descriptions. You have got to be kidding me. "Lined in peach faille." I don't even know what "faille" is. So I flipped over my *I Sell* sheet and of course it was written up in my mother's handwriting. She is the one with a master's degree in home economics.

And boy, does she do great write-ups for fashion-forward items like these purses! I had bought these two purses at an estate sale of a purse collector. I paid way more than usual, but figured it would   be a learning experience. And at $25 each, I knew that if I started each auction at $24.99, I couldn't lose any real money.

The 1950s and 1960s in America were a time of huge fashion statements. One of the premier items was the Lucite handbag. What does "Lucite handbag" even mean?

Lucite was developed in the 1950s by DuPont, and it turned out that this wonderful new plastic was ideal for making boxy-style handbags. It was high-quality plastic and could be made in an opaque or translucent color. It could also be molded and carved into shapes never seen before.

The plastic could be marbleized or pearlized, and decorations were easy to add; almost anything imaginable could be glued onto the surface. Things like flowers, shells, confetti, and rhinestones were used to make these purses even more fancy.

I think now that the copper purse that sold for $102.30 to an Austrian buyer was probably marbleized, and I had called it pearlized. The other one I sold was made by Florida Handbags; it went to Belgium with a selling price of $81, but I correctly called that one pearlized. It also had a cut-out diamond decoration.

During the '50s and '60s, these purses were all the rage in major cities like New York, Miami and Los Angeles. The best of the designers and the names to look for are Wilardy of New York, Gilli Originals, Charles Kahn, Patricia of Miami, Stylecraft of Miami, Evans, Lewellyn, Myles, Maxim, Tyrolean, and Rialto.

These upper-end companies marked their bags with a stamp on the metal frame or a clear label. Over the years, many of these clear labels have fallen off, which can make identification difficult.

You may want to pay for an appraisal if you think you have an upper-end bag that is unmarked.

As with any type of purse, these handbags were available in different degrees of quality and price. They were a fun fashion statement, and so unusual that they are very collectible today—especially for those who love vintage fashion accessories.

Oh, yeah—"faille" is a fabric that has a crosswise rib which makes it drape very well; it's finer than grosgrain, but in the same family. What I think is even stranger than "faille" is that both these purses went to Europe, and my favorite purse that I carried as a small child in the late 1960s came from Europe. It was pink vinyl with bells on it. I still have it (imagine that)!

#54 Caithness Paperweight

$3.00
Paid

From: Estate sale

Caithness Starlight Scotland Art Glass Paperweight Blk

Description:
Great Scottish paperweight is black and white with controlled bubbles—clear glass. Beautiful. 2.5" by 3". N64363 and signed "Caithness."

Winning Bid:

$100.00

Ended: 3/3/07
History: 24 bids
Starting Bid: $9.99
Winner: Columbia, MO

Viewed

000161 X

Caithness Paperweight #54

The Story

Any time I find a signed paperweight that looks to be good quality for under $20, I usually grab it. This paperweight was made in Scotland and it was only $3. I didn't do any research before listing this item. What was the point? It was signed and I could easily identify it. You can't be a perfectionist and make a full-time living on eBay. I'm definitely NOT a perfectionist. My brother Lee, in fact, tells me, "You don't get caught up in the details. You are a go-getter, and you just push through when you need to."

I think Lee recognizes the qualities in me that have helped me succeed on eBay. My brother is an integral part of my business, and I am very fortunate to have his help. We have always been good friends, and I think (based on this Christmas photo) you can see that we were both destined to be involved with "The Queen of Auctions." I have no clue why we were wearing those crazy crowns!

The area where I just "push through" in my eBay business is in the listing process. I get frustrated when I am trying to teach eBay sellers to list quickly, and instead they want to make each listing as exquisite as possible. They do too much research, spend too much time revising and proofreading their writeups, and sink hours of time into decorative graphics.

The details can paralyze you and keep you from making a REAL living on eBay. Your goal is to list as many items as you can in an hour. My record is 67! You should be shooting for fifteen to twenty per hour. If it isn't up for sale, how can it sell? If it can't sell, how can you make a living?

Two days into the auction for this paperweight, it was bid up to over $220. At that point, I decided to do some research. I got on PriceMiner.com and found that the highest recent sales price for this item was $48.50. I also learned that Caithness is known for its high quality paperweights and art glass. They have been in business since 1961 and they take their inspiration from the colors of the Scottish landscape: warm peaty tones, purple heather, golden sunsets, and the grey blue of the lochs. Pretty cool! They are still in business today.

I couldn't figure out why mine was worth so much. Then I got an email from eBay that said an incorrect bid had been placed and it had been retracted. The buyer wanted to type in $80.00 but instead typed in $8,000.00, so he retracted his bid. Bummer!

My point is that I didn't do the research until I realized that I might have a special item. I also didn't spend time writing about the paperweight company or how many of this style were made and the item's original retail price. I did find that the original retail on this item was $85—but if I had put that into the description, it may not have sold for as much as it did.

Even with the bid retraction, this piece went for a pretty penny! More than my research suggested. Did I need to take more time and write the perfect description? Obviously not, since it sold for $100. Don't be a perfectionist!

#55 Faience Salt & Pepper

$0.00
Paid
From: Gift

Quimper Faience Salt Pepper Shakers As Is Set French

Description:
Quimper Faience signed French pair of salt and pepper shakers.
Man on one and lady on the other. They are 3¼" tall and 1¼" wide.
These are AS IS. One is completely chipped at the base as you can
see in the photo and the other one has some nicks.

Winning Bid:

$27.⁵²

Ended: 3/3/07
History: 6 bids
Starting Bid: $9.99
Winner: Tuscaloosa, AL

Viewed

000032 X

Faience Salt & Pepper   #55

The Story

My mom was helping me go through my kitchen cupboards and weed out things I didn't need. Remember, she has a master's degree in home economics, and I don't cook. Home economics is a formal study that includes topics like interior design, cleaning, sewing, cooking, nutrition and family relationships. It was originally designed in the 1800s to ready young women to become wives and run their homes correctly. It is definitely not for me.

Anyway, my mom made three piles in my kitchen: trash, charity, and eBay. In the trash pile I spotted this salt and pepper shaker set that had been a wedding present to William and me from William's sister Pam. She is a perfectionist, and I knew that these were probably very expensive originally.

The set was completely "as is"—the base on the man was broken. But I told my mom there was no way I was throwing it out—it would definitely sell on eBay. My mom said, "Are you crazy?" "Yes, a little," I answered, "but I need you to write them up so I can list them."

My mom finally acquiesced and wrote them up!!! "Acquiesced" is such a great word—"accepted without protest." I would like to see more of that from my children. I bet if I had a home economics degree I would be running a tighter ship. Just kidding!

The company that made this set, the Faïencerie HB-Henriot, was founded in 1690 in Quimper, France. The original company wasn't called "HB" until one of the owner's daughters married Antoine de la Hubaudiere. Starting in 1771 it used the trademark HB (for la "Hubaudiere").

In 1776 and 1791, two other *faïenceries* started up in Quimper, directly competing with HB. These competing factories didn't decorate all their pieces, and when they did, the artists used their fingers (rather than brushes) to apply the paint, so most decorated pieces featured only very simple floral designs. In 1872, one of the new *faïenceries* hired an artistic director, Alfred Beau. He started using the famous design of the little Breton man and woman in their traditional headdress on his company's pieces.

That is what was on my salt and pepper shakers! In 1906, Henriot bought out the company that had hired the artistic director, leaving only two *faïenceries* to battle it out. The period between 1920 and 1940 was an intensely competitive time and both companies produced many great pieces.

In 1968, the two remaining companies merged into HB Henriot. The company is still in business today. Each piece of Quimper pottery is fully handmade and hand-painted. An HB Henriot piece should bear the "HB Henriot" signature along with the initials of the artist to ensure authenticity.

I would have been happy to have my "as is" salt and pepper shakers sell for $9.99, but as you can see, I got a lot more than that for them. And they got shipped to Tuscaloosa, Alabama. From France, to my wedding, to Tuscaloosa!

#56 Dahl Jensen Bull Dog

$20.00
Paid
From: Professional estate sale

Dahl Jensen Royal English Bull Dog Figurine Copenhagen

Description:
This is a darling figurine. Signed "Jens Peter Dahl Jensen DJ Copenhagen Denmark" in green. Style 1139 AP. Made sometime between 1928 and 1981. Puppy dog is ivory and brown and has so much character. 2½" by 2½".

Winning Bid: $192.51

Ended: 3/3/07
History: 14 bids
Starting Bid: $49.99
Winner: West Orange, NJ

Viewed
000233 X

Dahl Jensen Bull Dog #56

The Story

I saw this darling miniature bulldog figurine at an estate sale. It looked a lot like a Bing & Grondahl or a Royal Copenhagen piece, but it was signed "Jens Peter Dahl Jensen," which I had never heard of. However, it was still Danish and I have always had great luck with bulldogs. So I bought it for $20.

The bulldog is a small dog, very wide and compact, with a thick, massive head. The bulldog got its name in the British Isles because it was used to bait the bull before a fight (back when bullfighting was common in many parts of Europe). The original bulldog had to be ferocious, courageous, and insensitive to pain. When dog fighting became illegal in England, breeders set out to eliminate the dog's fierce qualities. What they ended up with is an excellent family pet.

The bulldog is gentle and protective. However, it is still quite bull-headed and determined. Bulldogs do not give up easily. The AKC (American Kennel Club) says that they are one of the most popular breeds due to their lovable disposition and adorable wrinkles.

I wish someone would think my wrinkles are adorable. Oh, well—there is botox for that. No wonder any bulldog item sells well.

As I was doing my research on Jens Peter Dahl Jensen, up came my friend Stan Tillotson's web site (http://stan.tillotson.com). Stan has been in the Danish porcelain business for decades, and I consider him an expert. He got to know my grandmother and me many years ago when we were selling Royal Copenhagen plates through the *Antique Trader*.

We did a lot of business over the years, with him in Florida and us in Bellingham. He even took a trip through Bellingham with his partner, Steve, and visited our shop to meet us in person. That was back in 1998.

What I found out about Jens Peter Dahl Jensen was very interesting. He was a Danish designer who lived from 1874 to 1960. He was trained as a sculptor at the Copenhagen Academy. In 1897, at the age of 23, he started working for Bing & Grondahl, where he stayed for twenty years as a designer. I just knew this dog looked like Bing & Grondahl!

Jens Peter spent another eight years as the artistic director at one of the Bing & Grondahl factories. In 1925, at age 51, he started his own factory in Copenhagen and earned recognition as the producer of the finest Danish porcelain figurines. The company continued producing its wares until 1984, when it finally closed its doors.

I was thrilled when my bulldog figurine sold for almost $200! It was also fun for me to catch up with my old friend Stan Tillotson. He is a wealth of knowledge and I encourage all of you to check out his website, which he built all by himself in 1998. Stan had his website almost completely finished when he suffered a major heart attack. He lost his memory of the previous three months, forgetting HTML, his passwords, and the programs he had used. But he got back to work, relearned everything, and finished the website. Just like a bulldog, Stan did not give up.

#57 Kodak Slide Trays

$0.00 Paid
From: Gift from my brother

Eastman Kodak Vintage Case 10 Slide Trays 80 Carousel

Description:
Each carousel slide tray holds 80 slides each. These are Eastman Kodak brand from the 1960s. They belonged to my parents and grandparents. This auction is for a case of 10. One of the boxes says "cat. 148 6232" on it. There are 7 black slide trays and 3 grey ones. There is some writing on some of the boxes and slight wear to the cardboard. The actual trays are in very good condition.

Winning Bid:

$49.99
Ended: 3/5/07
History: 1 bid (sold in store)
Starting Bid: $49.99
Winner: Louisville, KY

Viewed
 **X**

Kodak Slide Trays   #57

The Story

Wow! Did this item ever bring back memories? You know what we used to do as a family for fun? My grandpa or dad would haul out a screen and set it up in the living room. Then out would come cases and cases of carousel slide trays. I can still hear the hum of that machine's fan as my dad or grandpa would click the remote control button and we would watch slides of vacations past. This was apparently before DVD movie rentals!

We watched my grandmother's first trip to Europe in 1960. The family trip to Europe in 1969 (when Lee and I got to go). My first birthday. Lee's first birthday. Our trip back to Illinois to see the family farm. Etcetera, etcetera. At the very end of the slide show, there would only be a small handful of pictures of Kristin (my sister), and then the show was over.

The first round tray for slides was this carousel style. It came out in 1961 and was considered revolutionary! The Kodak carousel projector model 550 could hold 81 slides per tray and even came with a remote control. It is odd, but I have a Kodak model 760H carousel projector mint in box up for sale on eBay as I write this story, and it sold for $51.99 today! I only paid $5 for it at a garage sale.

But back to the carousel trays. My brother somehow inherited those cases and cases of slides. He decided to put all the slides in small photo-safe boxes, so he didn't need the carousels anymore. He gave them to me to sell on eBay. I started them at $9.99 in August of 2006, but they didn't sell. I was happy enough to wait until March of 2007 to get my full asking price of almost $50.

As these were being paid for, we were planning a huge surprise for my kids. Lee was actually in Disney World with Houston and Indy. My mom flew in that same day to surprise the kids. They didn't know she was coming. And (even crazier), I flew in two days later and was just standing in the lobby of their hotel when they came down for dinner. I think Houston tackled me to the ground, he was so excited, and Indy wouldn't stop hugging me.

I always tell them that I am too busy to go to Disney World with them— I have a book to write, or an ezine to publish. So it was an incredible treat for them, and an even bigger surprise was we were taking them on a four-day Disney cruise! I don't think they stopped grinning from ear to ear for the entire five days. It was a blast, and I was fortunate to be able to give them this treat.

We don't sit around our living room watching slides to reminisce about this wonderful 2007 trip. But we do get to watch an amazing DVD with photos and video that Lee put together with music. Technology has come such a long way! But taking the time to make the memories is what matters— not how you view them.

#58 Owl Coffee Mug

$2.00 Paid
From: Estate sale

Funky Eames Era Portugal Secia Owl Coffee Mug MOD P249

Description:
This interesting coffee mug is signed with "Secia Made in Portugal" and "P249" for a style number. Brownish green. So cute! In very good condition with no chips, no cracks, no crazing. Needs slight cleaning. Very 1950s 1960s.

Winning Bid: $25.48

Ended: 3/21/07
History: 5 bids
Starting Bid: $9.99
Winner: Palm Coast, FL

Viewed
 000059 X

Owl Coffee Mug #58

The Story

I got a very disturbing phone call two days before this owl coffee mug sold. It was from Ann Brown's son Mark, to let us know that she had passed away. Ann was my mother's cousin. Her dad was my grandmother's brother Houston Sussex and her mother was Josephine Simas, who was Portuguese. We have a very small family on my mother's side, so the news was a shock.

It was quite a shock to Ann's entire family also. We decided to drive to Bakersfield, CA that Friday for the funeral.

My mom and I planned to pick up Ann's sister, Gwen, in Desert Hot Springs at 6:30 am to arrive in Bakersfield in time for the service. Ann's death was especially hard on Gwen, as now she had no living full siblings left. Ann was the firstborn; after her came Clive, and twins Gwen and Gordon were last.

When Ann was about four years old, her mother left her in the back yard with two-year-old Clive. He tripped and fell into a stream and drowned. Ann never got over feeling responsible—but of course, it was NOT her fault. Then, at age 21, Gordon lost his life in a tragic boating accident trying to save a fishing boat at the mouth of the Columbia river when he was a member of the Oregon Coast Guard.

My grandmother said that her brother, Houston, never got over losing both of his sons to drowning. She said he took to the seas in his sailboat "The Balea" (Portuguese for "whale") and never came back. He was obsessed with the ocean. Many years later, Houston did have a third son, Renato, with his second wife.

It was strange to me that this Portuguese mug sold on the day of Ann's funeral, especially since Ann was half Portuguese, and owls in many cultures signify death and doom.

The Aztecs and Mayans considered the owl a symbol of death and destruction. There is an old saying in Mexico that, "When the owl sings, someone dies." The Romanians think that the call of the owl means that someone in their neighborhood is going to die. In France, they make a distinction between eared owls (which are symbols of wisdom) and owls without visible ears (which are considered birds of bad omen).

Ann's service was beautiful, and we spent the afternoon at her home with our extended family mourning her passing. Ann was a talented artist who ran a very interesting home. She never owned a washer or dryer, choosing instead to do all her laundry by hand, letting it dry outside on the clothesline. She also allowed no Internet in her house. Her home was beautiful, sleek, and mid-century and reminded me of simpler times—just like this owl mug was from the simpler times of that same era, the 1950s. Ann is dearly missed.

#59   RS Prussia Pot and Cups

$85.⁰⁰/6
Paid
From: Church sale

RS Prussia Antique Chocolate Pot Cocoa MW Handpainted

Description:

This lovely piece is signed "RS Germany" in the green backstamp with a star. Also signed with a handpainted "MW" and what looks like an "E." 9.5" by 7" to handle. Excellent condition. No chips, no cracks, no crazing. Greens, golds, browns. Water lilies, dogwood or flower. We have the matching demitasse chocolate cup and saucers up for sale in separate auctions. I would guess 1920s.

Winning Bid: **$239.⁹⁵/6**

Ended: 3/24/07
History: 22 bids/6
Starting Bid: $99 pot/$9.99 ea c/s
Winner: Texas, Poland

Viewed
 X

RS Prussia Pot and Cups #59

The Story

I was at one of my favorite church sales and this set was marked $170. The ladies at this church sale know me and are good to me. It was the second day of the sale and they let me have it for $85. I know that is a lot to pay, but it is the church where Indy went to pre-school and with whom we have gone on missions to Mexico; I knew the money was going to a great cause.

Speaking of Indy, she had started singing with a very fancy children's choir in the fall of 2006—the Desert Chorale Concert Children's Choir. She actually had to audition. She loved being a part of it and stayed for two years. This fancy chocolate pot set was selling on the day that Indy's choir was asked to perform on our local CBS Channel 2 news station.

It was very exciting. She had to be in the studio at 6 am. They were going on TV to promote their spring concert. I was so proud of her!

But back to the Prussia set. Can you imagine owning something so beautiful that was just used to serve chocolate? You would have also owned a coffee pot and a tea pot. A chocolate pot is typically taller and thinner than a coffee pot. A tea pot is the shortest and widest of the three. Those times are long gone. Now we just throw whatever it is we want into a coffee mug and start the microwave—or drive through for it!

Prussia was a former kingdom in northern Europe; it covered an area that today includes parts of Germany and Poland. RS (Reinhold Schlegelmilch) Prussia is very collectible. I remember my grandmother al-ways telling me about them, and telling me to look for the mark and always note if it green or red. I think she told me the green mark was better.

A chocolate pot was used for serving hot chocolate. The first chocolate drink was created by the Mayans more than 2,000 years ago. It was very bitter. It became a staple of the Aztec culture by the 1400s. After winning a war against the Aztecs, Cortes demanded all their valuables. One of those valuables was, of course, the bitter chocolate drink. Cortes returned to Spain in 1528 and he brought cocoa beans and the drink-making equipment with him to Europe.

The drink slowly gained popularity. The first recorded commercial shipment of cocoa to Europe sailed from Veracruz, Mexico to Seville, Spain in 1585. The Europeans started adding sugar to the chocolate to counteract its natural bitterness. Hot chocolate became a luxury item among the European nobility beginning in the seventeenth century. It was sweet, but very expensive—chocolate cost $60 a pound in the 1600s!

All five of the cup and saucers sold for $20.49 each and went to Poland. This makes perfect sense, now that I know that northern Poland was originally part of the Kingdom of Prussia. The chocolate pot sold for $137.50 and went to San Antonio, Texas. I was happy to make about $155 on this in one week—I tripled my money. And we are hoping that someday Indy will be a triple threat: singer, dancer, and actress!

#60 Michelangelo Turtle Bowl

$0.⁰⁰ **Paid**

From: Came with cereal

Michelangelo Teenage Mutant Ninja Turtles Bowl 1990 WOW

Description:
Plastic bowl is green and says "Michelangelo Teenage Mutant Ninja 1990" on it. 6.5" by 5" by 2". Wear and needs cleaning.

Winning Bid:

$9.⁹⁹

Ended: 3/25/07
History: 1 bid
Starting Bid: $9.99
Winner: PA

Viewed
 X

Michelangelo Turtle Bowl #60

The Story

When I started dating William (who would become my husband), we got a kitten together. He was an orange tabby named "Kerouac" (after the author Jack Kerouac), and he was completely crazy. He would walk the railing on the third level of our townhouse and even sleep up there. It must have been 50 feet high. He had no fear.

Kerouac was a great cat and moved with us from LA to Bellingham and finally to Palm Desert in 2002. I had kitty doors put into this house so he could come and go as he pleased. One day I came home and found that a strange cat had used those kitty doors and was exploring the eBay room. It freaked Kerouac out.

That was in 2006, and he was fifteen years old. He started marking his territory all over the house after that incident. It was not pretty. I took him to the vet, who suggested we put him on kitty Valium. I didn't think so. A year later, his health had deteriorated even more. My dad was visiting, and Kerouac began throwing up blood all over the house.

My dad looked at me and said, "It is time. Do you want me to take care of him?" I was completely bawling my head off. Even though he had been kind of a burden that last year, we still loved him. Thank God my dad was here that week to arrange for Kerouac to be put down. I kept his little kitty collar, but started to throw the rest of his stuff away.

This green turtle bowl had held Kerouac's food for the past twelve years. As I was about to toss it into the trash can, I pulled my hand back. The thought occurred to me that maybe I could sell it on eBay. Sick and wrong? Probably, but I listed it that week and it sold for $9.99 to a buyer in Pennsylvania.

Who would spend $10 for a green plastic Teenage Mutant Ninja Turtle bowl with twelve years of wear on it? It had to be a die-hard fan of the Teenage Mutant Ninja Turtles (TMNT). The TMNT were animated characters who lived in the storm sewers of Manhattan and battled criminals, evil superheroes, and alien invaders. They started out as cartoon characters in comic books and then became a TV series. After that, an action figure line was developed, and there was even a TMNT movie!

The TMNT became a part of pop culture history (just as the author Jack Kerouac had). At the height of TMNT's popularity (the late 1980s), you could buy TMNT items ranging from Pez dispensers to bedspreads. I don't remember where we got this bowl, but I am guessing it came as a giveaway with some sort of breakfast cereal. It featured the character "Michelangelo," who wore an orange bandanna and carried nunchucks. He was the easy-going, free-spirited turtle of the gang. He was funny and he liked to relax, but he also had an adventurous side.

My little Kerouac was a lot like Michelangelo. He was adventurous and loved to relax (sleep a lot)—at least until that other cat invaded his space. Too bad Kerouac didn't have his nunchucks on him that day, or he would have made quick work of that invader. I know Kerouac is in a better place now—and so is his bowl.

#61 Heller Plastic Dishes

$3.⁰⁰/12
Paid
From: Thrift store

Hot Pink Square Tray Plate Heller Massimo Vignelli RARE

Description:

9¾" square. Melmac Eames-era design. No chips, no cracks. In good to excellent condition with slight scratching—hardly noticeable. This hot pink color is very hard to find. We have a lot of Heller pieces up for sale this week. We got an incredible collection. All are signed "Heller." The pink also have "Designed by Massimo Vignelli." The purple pieces do not say that but are also signed "c Heller Mamaronek, NY manufactured under license for JMS products Christ Church NZ."

Winning Bid:

$91.⁸⁸/12

Ended: 4/3/07
History: 12 bids/12 (auction & store)
Starting Bid: $9.99 ea ($6.49 store)
Winner: Japan, Australia, KY, FL, MA, MN, WI

Viewed
000201 X

Heller Plastic Dishes #61

The Story

Juliette (one of my best friends from college) had been staying at her in-laws' house here in the desert for Easter. She went to thrift stores with me one day and I found this amazing set of Massimo Vignelli Heller for only $3. Yippee! Score! Juliette is very interested in eBay and thrift store shopping, but has never taken the plunge to sell on her own, probably because her kids are still pretty little—six and four that week.

What great Easter colors this set was. Hot pink and purple. I had never seen this type of tray in those bright, wild colors before, and never in square shapes. How exciting. I listed them at auction right away at $9.99 each. Four of the auctions sold with bids. I moved the remaining eight plates into my eBay store at a fixed price of $9.99 each.

Unfortunately, I was testing eBay's markdown manager that week and I did a "35% off collectibles" category sale. The eight store listings for these plastic dishes sold within hours at $6.49 each. Oh well, live and learn. I still brought in $91.88 on a $3 investment within eight days!

Heller began in 1971 in Australia and its very first product line was the stacking melamine dishes designed by Massimo Vignelli. Massimo is a famous Italian designer who was born in 1931 in Milan and currently still has a design house in NY City.

But what really intrigued me with all of this was the question, "Just what is melamine and why is it different than Melmac?" I often get those two terms confused. Melamine resin is a hard, plastic material made from melamine and formaldehyde. Melamine dishes are NOT microwave safe, as they heat up from the microwaves. Melamine is a heat cured material—once set, it can never be melted and can NOT be recycled. It was first developed in the 1940s. It is easily molded into different shapes and is durable. It was great for households with children. No breakage!

Melmac is a trade name for melamine. So they are the same thing! Cool! Starting in the 1950s, Melmac dinnerware could be found in almost every kitchen in the US. Any color pigment could be added. Popular colors in the 1950s were sea foam or pea green; the 1960s brought more psychedelic shades. Melmac was also used to make those hideous trays we used in the school cafeteria. By the end of the 1970s, Melmac's popularity began to wane due to its tendency to scratch and stain.

Juliette and I shared an apartment for six years after college. We were very compatible roommates. She was a perfectionist. If we had any Melmac dinnerware in our shared kitchen and it got a scratch on it, Juliette would have thrown it away in a New York second. That is why Melmac in great condition brings in the big bucks on eBay. Watch out for those perfectionist types—they can ruin our eBay successes.

#62 Filson Jacket

$5.⁰⁰
Paid
From: Charity sale

Filson 865 Original Wool Shirt Mens M Navy Burgundy

Description:
This is a great shirt that can be worn as a light jacket. Filson has
been in business since 1897. 25" Sleeve and 48" chest. 20" center
back. In excellent condition and it looks new to me but no tags.
Original wool shirt straight collar in burgundy and navy blue plaid.
Keeps you warm even when wet. 100% Merino virgin wool.

Winning Bid:

$66.⁰¹
Ended: 4/8/07
History: 6 bids
Starting Bid: $9.99
Winner: Saskatchewan,
Canada

Viewed
000152 X

Filson Jacket #62

The Story

It was Easter week and my mom and I were out yard saling. We found an awesome sale that had tons of designer clothes. That is really my mom's area of expertise, so I just hung back, helped her where I could, and checked out the men's rack.

She was so focused on the woman's clothing that I had the men's table all to myself. I found a gorgeous orange and white pinstripe suit shirt for Houston. He had insisted on a white suit for Easter and this shirt was the perfect complement for only $2. Indy always looks pretty in the Easter dresses that she picks out.

I also found this Filson shirt jacket for $5. It looked brand new and reminded me of the spiffy Pendleton jackets that my grandfather wore. He was a hunter and loved his Pendletons. My mom didn't mind at all that I bought this one to sell on eBay, as she had already bought 70 pieces of clothing for $500.

It turned out that I was correct in thinking this jacket resembled Pendleton. Filson's motto is "might as well have the best." The Filson company is based in Seattle, Washington, and Pendleton is based in Portland, Oregon—about three hours apart by car.

C.C. Filson was born in 1850 and inherited his father's pioneer spirit. I would think that anyone born in 1850 would have had to be a pioneer. Anyway, after homesteading in Nebraska, he moved to the small (at the time) city of Seattle in the 1890s.

It turns out he had great timing. In 1897, the Klondike Gold Rush started and thousands of fortune hunters were heading to Seattle on their way to Canada. It is strange, but when I was little, we lived in Canada (Edmonton, Alberta) for four years while my dad taught at the University of Alberta. We used to have to get dressed up in funny Gold Rush outfits (that my mom made) every summer and go to the Klondike Days celebration!

When the gold rush hit, C.C. Filson had been running a loggers' outfitting store for a few years, and he was ready to take his business to the next level. In 1897, he opened a store in the area now known as Pioneer Square named "CC Filson's Pioneer Alaska Clothing and Blanket Manufacturers." It specialized in tough, comfortable clothing for hunters, fishermen, explorers, and miners.

Even after the Gold Rush ended, Filson kept listening to his customers. If he didn't stock an item a customer needed, he would custom make it for them. The Filson name became synonymous with reliability, satisfaction, and honest values. It is still considered a top-of-the-line brand.

I made over $60 on this jacket. That sure helped pay for our Easter brunch at Desert Willows Golf Course. It was a lovely Easter, I had two well-dressed kids, and our brunch was delicious. However, I don't know if they were as snappy looking as we were for the Klondike Days celebration!

#63 Pottery Barn Canoe

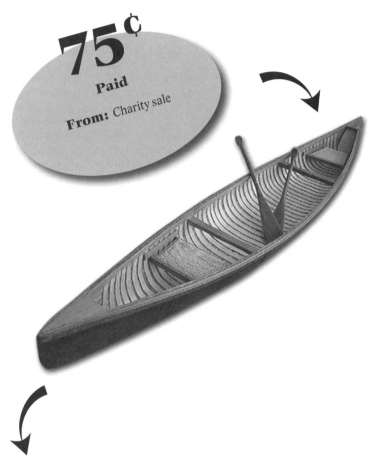

75¢
Paid
From: Charity sale

Pottery Barn Long Canoe 2 Paddles Darling Décor Boat AM

Description:
Darling Canoe is 30" long by 4½" by 2". It is signed "Pottery Barn AM." One of the paddles has been broken and needs some glue. This is such a darling piece of home décor.

Winning Bid: **$34.³³**

Ended: 4/12/07
History: 9 bids
Starting Bid: $9.99
Winner: Normal, IL

Viewed

000134 X

Pottery Barn Canoe #63

The Story

I found this darling canoe for 75 cents at a charity sale. You should never pass up a decent piece of Pottery Barn when it is that cheap!

Pottery Barn, as you probably know, is an American-based chain of home décor stores (over 200 stores plus an awesome catalog) that is based in San Francisco. It is now a fully-owned subsidiary of Williams-Sonoma (remember story #9?). But Pottery Barn has a really neat history behind it.

It was founded by Paul Secon and his brother Morris in 1949. The story goes that Morris' wife bought some stoneware at a yard sale (too cool—I didn't know they had yard sales in the 1940s!) in Rochester, New York. The pieces were designed by Glidden Parker, and Morris took an instant liking to them. He contacted Parker and Parker told him that he had three barns full of discontinued or slightly damaged product for sale.

I bet you can see where this is going. Pottery, barns, a business.... So Morris called his brother Paul, who was a very talented musician. He was a music editor for Billboard and was also a songwriter for Nat King Cole. When Morris told him that they could buy all the pieces for $2,500, the brothers decided to go for it. With the help of their father, they rented a store in Lower Manhattan, NY to sell their new stock. Pottery Barn was started! The company eventually based its philosophy on the fact that home furnishings should be exceptional in comfort, style and quality.

As this darling Pottery Barn piece was selling I was boarding a flight to Nicaragua. What an adventure! I was still working madly on my *3rd 100 Best* book, but Peter and I decided to go down and check out a development that my friend owned and see about purchasing some land.

We were headed to the sleepy fishing village of San Juan del Sur and we didn't land in Managua until midnight. My friend's brother-in-law picked us up and we drove until 3 am, when we arrived at our eco-friendly hotel. Let me tell you that an eco-friendly hotel is not for Peter nor me. This hotel had no electricity (read "no air conditioning") and the trip to our room required us to walk about a mile across rope bridges. It was literally 100 degrees and humid. We both thought we were going to die.

This eco-friendly hotel was also not cheap at $300 a night. We toughed it out that night, but the next morning we checked ourselves in to the Piedras y Olas. Our new hotel was not green, but it was friendly, with three swimming pools, two bars, two restaurants, views of the ocean, and not a single rope bridge, all for only $80 a night. That was more like it!

Peter and I did end up buying some land in San Juan del Sur. That investment turned out to be a big mistake when the banks started going under here in the US. It is too bad, because I could see us decorating our ocean-view vacation home with a canoe just like this one.

However, spending 75-cents for this canoe turned out much better than the Nicaraguan investment. I made 45 times my initial purchase price in just seven days. I am going to stick with eBay from here on out!

#64 Antique Ruby Ring

$0.00 Paid
From: Inheritance

14k Yellow Gold Antique 1920's Art Deco Ring Ruby NICE

Description:
This is a very nice antique ring. I would guess the 1920s. Fine and thin band. It has been worn and it has an etched design and a ruby stone. The size is 8 to 8.25. My brother is a gemologist and he checked it all out for me. Marked 14k.

Winning Bid: **$69.99**
Ended: 4/29/07
History: 1 bid (sold in store)
Starting Bid: $69.99
Winner: Ft. Lauderdale, FL

Viewed
 000532 X

Antique Ruby Ring #64

The Story

My grandma was very interested in birthstones. She was born in January (like my brother) so their birth stone is garnet. Indiana is December, so her birthstone is blue topaz. Houston and I are July, so our birthstone is ruby.

A ruby is an amazing stone. Its rich red color signifies love and passion. The word comes from the Latin *"Ruber"* which means "red." It is a variety of the mineral corundum and is mined from metamorphic rock. Corundum is the second hardest mineral (after diamond). Corundum comes in a variety of colors, but is only called a ruby when it is red. In any other color it is called a "sapphire."

The ancient Hindus called the ruby "King of Gems." Is that like "Queen of Auctions"? (Just kidding.) The ruby is one of the most highly prized gems in history. It was thought to have magical powers and was worn by royalty as a protection against evil. Stories were told saying it would turn a darker red when danger was approaching; once the person wearing it was safe, it would return to its original color—as long as it was in the possession of the rightful owner. Wild!

I think I need some rubies. I do have a ruby cross from my grandmother, but the chain broke. As I was working on this story, I put my ruby cross on another chain, so I can finish this story.

Rubies were mined starting more than 2,500 years ago. The Burmese ruby is especially prized, but many other wonderful rubies come from Sri Lanka, India, Australia, Kenya, Tanzania, and even the U.S. My grandmother traveled to Sri Lanka on numerous occasions to buy gems. She loved to do that. I always admired her so much for following her passion, and those passions made her money.

Even though ruby wasn't my grandmother's birthstone, I think she liked rubies even more than diamonds. This neat antique ring sold out of my eBay store on a Sunday in April, when Houston was having a one-hour baseball lesson with Mark Cresse.

Mark Cresse is an awesome coach; you may recognize his name for many reasons! He was a bullpen coach for the LA Dodgers for over 20 years, and he now runs baseball camps in Orange County, CA. During 2006, Houston trained quite a bit with Mark. On the Sunday that this ring sold, my mom, Lee, and Indy joined me to watch Houston working with Mark. It was so much fun! As we left, Houston said, "His metaphors really make sense." My ten-year-old knew exactly what a metaphor is; I would have said examples instead of metaphors.

Unfortunately, Cresse moved out of the desert, and Houston doesn't get to train with him anymore. Bummer! We miss that gem of a coach. By the way, an hour with Cresse (way back when) was $70. Do you think that my grandma was helping Houston and I out with this $69.99 sale on that same day? I think so.

#65 Parrot Lamp & Golfer Statue

$2.⁵⁰/2 Paid
From: Garage sale

**1970's Bizarre Op Art Campy Woman Golfer Lamp Big Boobs
Parrot Lamp on Perch Light Plastic Tropical Fun Darling**

Descriptions:

This is such a campy golf statue. It is a lamp base. Very strange. 16"
by 6½". Plaster. There is wear to the paint and small nicks but overall in great shape. Bright green and yellow. Signed on the back with
"Bobbie Michael McKie." This piece is great. Needs cleaning.

This is a really fun parrot lamp. He lights up and really works. Needs
slight cleaning but otherwise in great condition. Style 52350. 13½"
by 5". Cute!

Winning Bid: $39.⁹⁸/2

Ended: 5/7/07
History: 1 bid ea (sold in store)
Starting Bid: $24.99/$14.99
Winner: Lake Mary, FL

Viewed

000296 X

Parrot Lamp & Golfer Statue #65

The Story

These were two of the campiest items I had ever purchased. Just what is "campy"? The correct term is "camp," and the first recorded use of the word dates it to 1909. Can you believe that? It is defined as a term for "something that becomes appealing because of its bad taste and ironic value."

The term has changed over the years. In 1909 it meant "ostentatious, exaggerated, affected and theatrical," but by the middle of the 1970s it was used to describe "mediocrity and ostentations so extreme that they have a perverse sophisticated appeal." It is a little hard to get a handle on, but it seems that camp style became popular in the 1980s with the widespread adoption of postmodern views on art and culture.

Postmodernism is the style that developed after the Eames era which was a mid-century modern look. During the Eames era everything was sleek, futuristic, and minimalistic. I would say that the end of the 1960s into the early 1980s would be the postmodern era, where we reverted back to excess, overspending and extravagance. "Camp" just may be the term we have been searching for to define the 1980s!

What is really bizarre (and notice that I did spell bizarre correctly this time) is that the parrot lamp was listed to end at auction on April 19, 2007, but did not sell. We relisted it in our eBay store immediately after, at $14.99, and it sold on May 7th, less than three weeks later. The beauty of the entire transaction is this.

The lady who bought the campy parrot lamp also bought the campy big-boobed (can I say that?) golfer lady that had been in my eBay store since February 17th of 2005—over two years! I honestly thought the golfer was never going to bring in the $24.99 I was asking. But there was just something so weird and cool and "camp" about her. Don't forget, "strange sells."

I like the word "camp" and think that in a sense my *100 Best* books are "camp." They take a fun and not serious approach to eBay as a business. I even think that eBay is a bit "camp." As I was selling these two items to Florida—a perfect location for a camp golfing statue and light-up parrot—my third *100 Best* book was finally finished and handed off to the printer. What a relief! I loved our new title *(Ka-Ching!),* which even sounds like a camp term.

#66 Pewter Dragon Stein

Pewter Stein BMF Dragon German Vintage NEAT Siegfrieds

Description:
This amazing stein with hinged lid is signed with "BMF" and "95%"
I think. Dragon on it. Words written look like "Kompf Mit Dom
Dracken Siegfrieds Tod Vikings Schalsd Michelanger." 6½" by 5½".
Excellent condition.

Winning Bid:

$76.00
Ended: 5/15/07
History: 10 bids
Starting Bid: $9.99
Winner: Brooklyn, NY

Viewed
 X

Pewter Dragon Stein   #66

The Story

I found this darling stein at a garage sale for $1. Can't pass up a pewter beer stein for that price, can you? I listed it on eBay without doing any research. You know my style at this point—minimal research. It ended up selling for 76 times my initial investment, so I had to include it in this book and find out why? Oh why?

Let's start with the difference between a beer mug and a beer stein. Mugs do not have lids, and steins do. Steins typically sell for more than mugs. The word "stein" (of course) is of German origin, and comes from either "Stein Krug" (stone jug) or "Steingut" (stone goods). Steins were used for drinking beer (surprise, surprise!), and can be made from stoneware, pewter, wood, ceramic, crystal, porcelain, creamware, silver or glass.

Steins can be traditional, military, occupational, character (figural), or relief (bas design), and are frequently decorated according to a theme (think Christmas, wildlife, game fish, sports, dogs, military and other holidays). They range in size from 1 ounce (.03 liter) to 8.4 gallons (32 liters). Can you imagine drinking 8.4 gallons of beer? I think that could kill a person. The most common size is 16.9 ounces, or half a liter. Most steins have the liter mark to the left hand side of the handle. I used to like beer when I lived in Brentwood after college—Amstel Light was my favorite. I don't really drink beer anymore. Maybe I need to try it out of a stein.

Steins originated in the fourteenth century, when (because of the bubonic plague and infestations of flies in Europe) Germany made laws requiring beverage containers to have covers to stop the spread of disease. At that same time, stoneware was invented. So for the next 300 years there was an influx of steins with lids.

After doing my research, I still couldn't find out why this stein sold for so much. I decided to pay $9.95 for an online appraisal from WhatsItWorthToYou.com. Here is what they told me: "The text means 'the death of Siegfried,' 'the fight with the dragon,' and finally 'the treasure of another tribe.' Current fair market value for this stein is $40, and the steins are still being manufactured by Bayrische Metal Fabrik (BMF) and are not overly scarce."

As Susan Thornberg, my editor, was checking this story, she told me why this stein sold for so much. Yippeee! She said that the text on the stein includes references to a series of operas called the Ring Cycle.

The Ring Cycle was composed by Richard Wagner (VOG-ner) over a period of 26 years (from 1848 to 1874). The operas were based on an old myth called the Nibelung, which is sort of a German King Arthur story featuring Siegfried (lucky I had that name in my title) and Brunnhilde.

According to Susan, people who like Wagner *really* like Wagner. She had a friend in Boston who listened to Wagner's final opera "Parsifal" in its entirety EVERY DAY for over a year. It is about four hours long. In other words, Wagner fans get kind of fanatical about him. Fanatical enough to pay almost twice retail for a Wagner-themed stein—lucky for me! Thanks, Susan!

#67 Adams Cockfighting Pitcher

$7.00
Paid
From: Charity sale

Adams Old English Sports Cockfighting Cockfight Pitcher

Description:
This a great old English piece. England. 4" by 5". Signed with "Adams Old English Sports England" and "Drawn by H. Alken Cock Fight." Shows roosters fighting. Creamer or pitcher. In great condition. No chips, no cracks.

Winning Bid:

$86.50

Ended: 5/15/07
History: 4 bids
Starting Bid: $9.99
Winner: UK

Viewed
 X

Adams Cockfighting Pitcher #67

The Story

I paid $7 for this at a charity sale. I don't know why I did. That is beyond my typical $5 limit, but I had a feeling. Do you ever get those feelings? I hope you do, because they are priceless!

Priceless also describes this past week with my family. My mom is here for spring break and my brother came out for the weekend. It has been a blast. I just went outside where they are all playing in the pool, and I put my feet in. My mom said, "Come on in for a dip." I said, "There is no way, I have to write about a pitcher." She thought I was talking about Houston, the pitcher! We laughed, and here I am back inside writing about this amazing pitcher.

The pitcher had roosters on the front, but when I bought it I didn't realize that they were fighting. Amazing! Cockfighting was a blood sport between two roosters that was held in a ring called a cockpit. I think I should modify that "was" to "is," because I think cockfighting still goes on in various places (legally or not!).

It is currently illegal in the US and most of Europe. The gamecocks used in cockfights are specially bred birds that are conditioned to be very strong and have a lot of stamina. They are also bred to be aggressive toward all males of the same species. They are given the best of care until the age of two and groomed just like professional athletes prior to their games. This really made me think of Houston the pitcher. Anyway, cockfighting is a sick "sport," because most cocks die as a result of their fighting, even though cockfights are not fought to the death. But even if they don't actually die in the ring, these poor roosters sustain serious damage. It is a gambling event for the humans and an inhumane event for the animals.

Even though cockfighting was banned in England in 1835, it was considered an old English sport The Adams Company produced a line of china called "Old English Sports." I love the story of the Adams company. Two hundred years before it ever opened for business, two brothers, Adam and Richard, were fined for digging clay in the middle of an English street. No one knows if they were related to the company founders, but it makes for a great story!

In 1648, John Adams opened a pottery house in Staffordshire, England. The factory was eventually named the Greengates works and moved to Tunstall. The Adams company had a wonderful history of greatness throughout the centuries.

Sadly, on January 1, 1966, the company was bought out by Wedgwood. By 1992, Wedgwood decided to close the Greengates factory. When it closed, someone set fire to the property and it burned to the ground.

I would be devastated if my grandmother's store burned to the ground— all those lost memories! It's been hard enough to see the house taken over and changed by new owners. I can hardly ever drive by it because seeing it makes me so sad, but at least I have the option. And even though this rooster pitcher has long since been shipped to its buyer, I still I have an amazing pitcher in my family!

#68 Petites Choses Monkey

50¢
Paid
From: Garage sale

Monkey Wizard of Oz Masquerade Mardi Gras Petites Choses

Description:
This is the coolest monkey. Could be from the Wizard of Oz or Mardi Gras. Signed with the "Petites Choses" sticker. This is such a great piece. Monkey or gorilla with wings. Just like the Wizard of Oz flying monkeys. Wearing a mask, it has a candle holder base. 5½" by 4½". In great condition.

Winning Bid:

$20.⁵⁰

Ended: 5/15/07
History: 7 bids
Starting Bid: $9.99
Winner: St. Augustine, FL

Viewed
000062 X

Petites Choses Monkey #68

The Story

So weird typing in this description because we had just finished seeing *Wicked* in LA as this was selling. Selling a flying monkey while being at the Pantages Theater in Hollywood watching *Wicked* makes perfect eBay sense!

This monkey was signed "Petites Choses." I have had Petites Choses items before and they are mostly metal figurines and they sell well. *"Petites Choses"* means "little things" in French. I couldn't find out anything about the company, but that didn't matter since flying monkeys are apparently quite collectible.

Flying or winged monkeys were characters from *The Wonderful Wizard of Oz* and had enough exposure through the books and the 1939 movie to earn their place in popular culture. They were usually used as a comedic source of evil or fear. Kind of "camp," don't you think?

In the Oz novels, the monkeys could talk and were quite intelligent. They were controlled by a golden hat that was initially worn by the Wicked Witch of the West. In the classic 1939 movie, *The Wizard of Oz,* the monkeys are intelligent and obey commands, but do not speak. They are more animalistic and scary and only obey the Wicked Witch of the West. Boy, did that movie scare me when I was a kid.

Wicked, the musical, is the Wizard of Oz story told from the perspective of the witches. It takes place before Dorothy's arrival from Kansas. It is a fantastic play and the North American tour has been seen by over two million people. The show was nominated for ten 2004 Tony Awards and it won three. It was a great show and we enjoyed seeing it immensely.

Monkeys (even without wings) are quite collectible. Monkeys can be classified as either old world or new world and there are over 264 different species. Wow! Monkeys have been kept as pets through the years, and they range in size from only five inches long to three and a third feet long. They are omnivorous, and their diet consists of fruit, leaves, seeds, nuts, flowers, eggs and small animals (including insects and spiders).

When I was in Bali on my honeymoon, we visited the monkey forest. These forests, sacred to the Balinese, represent the harmonious coexistence of humans and nature. They are usually in sacred village areas, surrounded by temples. The monkey forest we saw was very beautiful and interesting— but a little creepy. The monkeys would come right up to us and we would feed them. Quite the experience!

The lady who bought this monkey just emailed me to tell why. "Dear Lynn, my guest bedroom has a monkey theme because of a great fabric I found. This monkey fit into the theme perfectly and is functional because it is a candleholder." Nice!

Selling this monkey for $20 more than I paid for it was also an experience and I got to remember my little friends in the Bali monkey forest. Remember that monkeys and *Petites Choses* (little things) sell!

#69 Golf Shirts

$51.^{00}/4
Paid
From: Garage sale

L Tommy Bahama Hawaiian Shirt Blue $110 Camp Kailua New

Description:
Brand new with the original tags. NWT/MWT. Blue with muted design. 100% silk. Island Etchings Camp Kailua 3343. Nice. We have a lot of great men's golf shirts up for sale this week. Most are cotton or silk and short sleeved. Retail ranges from $70.00 to $110.00. Check out our auctions for more great brand names .

Winning Bid:

$170.^{05}/4
Ended: 5/31/07
History: 42 bids/4
Starting Bid: $9.99
Winner: TX, FL, CA, PN

Viewed

000400 X

The Story

I was out garage saling with my mom in the state streets and we stumbled across a treasure trove of men's brand new golf shirts. The man selling them wanted $25 each to begin with and I talked him in to giving me six for $100. The retail prices ranged from $70 to $195. Can you believe that?

I bought 24 shirts, but as we drove away, I said to my mom, "I should go back and buy them all." So back we went (after getting another $300 cash from the ATM). There were 45 shirts remaining for which the seller wanted $700. I was ready to walk away until his mom (not my mom) talked him into $550. I ended up paying about $12.75 per shirt.

Included in the lot were shirts by all the big names in the golf industry. The shirts that sold for the most were the Tommy Bahamas. Tommy Bahama is a fictional character made up in 1992 by three retail gurus, two of which were Generra executives. Speaking of Generra, check me out in that 1980s Generra Hypercolor T-shirt with Juliette in story #61.

Story has it that they first conceived the Tommy Bahama brand while at their vacation homes on Florida's Gulf Coast. The name was meant to evoke a fictional character living the good life in the tropics and wearing classy, updated Hawaii shirts. You gotta love the concept! And apparently most people do.

The Tommy Bahama motto was "relax." Based in Seattle, Washington, the company started with just a single brand that was sold to upper-end department and specialty stores.

In 1995, Tommy Bahama opened its first retail shop near a Ritz Carlton in Naples, Florida. There are currently 40 Tommy Bahama locations, mostly in resort-type areas. Of course, we have one here in Palm Desert.

About the same time that they opened their first store, the founders were wondering how to get the most bang for their advertising buck. They asked themselves, "What would Tommy do?" Well, Tommy would have opened a brewpub and tropical café, and that is exactly what they did. There are about seven locations that have both the retail and the café. I love our Tommy Bahama restaurant here in the Valley.

The washable Tommy Bahama silk shirt really took off when Kevin Costner wore one in the movie *Tin Cup*. Juliette dated Kevin Costner for a while. This story seems to keep bringing me back to Juliette. As I was writing this, I was watching the auctions end on 25 used Tommy Bahama shirts I had listed for Juliette on eBay. They ended up selling for about $24 each! One that had an embroidered sailboat on the back just sold for $76! Never pass up Tommy Bahama.

I have shown you just a few of the new shirts here. Overall, on my $1,000 investment, I tripled my money—the shirts brought in about $3,000 total. While they were selling, I was on a plane headed to New York to autograph my new book, *Ka-Ching!,* and NOT to a tropical paradise where I could escape the troubles of my modern world. Relax!

#70 Cranberry Rose Bowl

$3.⁶⁰ Paid

From: Estate sale

Cranberry Glass Rose Bowl Leaves Satin Vintage Lovely

Description:
Raised pattern is clear and cranberry glass with satin type glass and leaves. Pressed glass. Needs cleaning. Rough around the opening at the top but no real chips, no cracks. 4½" by 4".

Winning Bid:

$64.⁰⁰

Ended: 6/13/07
History: 11 bids
Starting Bid: $9.99
Winner: New Albany, MS

Viewed

000127 X

Cranberry Rose Bowl #70

The Story

Mo had left in November of 2006 to start her own eBay business. Here we were in June of 2007 and I still didn't have an assistant. My mom was a great help, but I really needed to hire a permanent replacement for Maureen. That was not going to be easy. I put my usual ad on craigslist and got two candidates who sounded great. I set up interviews with both gals to meet at Wendy's. Only one of the girls showed up, and thank goodness she did! She was Carmen Badham.

My mom thought we should hire her on the spot. I thought we should be cautious, so I waited a few hours and then hired her. She is still here with us two years later. What a gem! She has a great sense of humor and gets along famously with Mo (who still stops by on occasion to lend a helping hand) and myself. Her husband, Jason, turned out to be a filmmaker, and he has done all of my DVDs and Boot Camps since then. How awesome did that turn out?

This was one of the first auctions that Carmen closed out for me. It was for a rose bowl in cranberry glass that I had bought when I got that huge house full of stuff. The price tag said $12, and I only paid 30% of that, or $3.60. It ended up selling for $64! Everyone should know what a rose bowl looks like and what it was used for. There are some serious rose bowl collectors out there.

Rose bowls were originally used in Queen Victoria's time (1837 to 1901), primarily in drawing rooms. A drawing room was a room in which visitors were entertained. It got its original name from the sixteenth-century term "withdrawing room." A withdrawing room was a room in which the owner of the house, his wife, or a distinguished guest could "withdraw" for more privacy. A drawing room today would be called a living room.

In the Victorian era, drawing rooms could get kind of musty. The Victorian drawing room usually had heavy drapes, musty fabrics, and lingering odors of pipe and wood smoke which did not make for a nicely scented space. Enter the rose bowl. It was half-filled with dried rose petals. In effect, it served as a potpourri. When the vase was set on a window or in the sun, the light shining through the petals was a beautiful and sweet-smelling sight.

Rose bowls are round in shape with a flat top and bottom. The top is usually cut out about 1½" to 3". Most have a crimped top with about eight waves, but some are flat like mine. Some are on pedestals, some have feet, and some can be more oval than round. True antique rose bowls can sell in the $50 to $1,000 range. Beware of reproductions. I got lucky when we hired Carmen—I got a perfect reproduction of Maureen. I didn't think such a thing existed!

#71 Carlton Ware Egg Cup

$2.00
Paid
From: Estate sale

Lustre Design Carlton Ware Pot Feet Salt Dip Egg Cup

Description:
What is this darling item? We have been told that it is probably an egg cup and it is so cute! 2½" by 2¾". Signed "England Carlton Ware" etc. Feet are green and gold. Little pot that could be a salt cellar, a toothpick holder or even a mustard. Very kitschy. Needs cleaning. No chips, no cracks, some crazing. Vintage.

Winning Bid: $29.02

Ended: 6/14/07
History: 7 bids
Starting Bid: $9.99
Winner: Australia

Viewed
 000085 X

Carlton Ware Egg Cup #71

The Story

This was selling as we were exhibiting in our booth at eBay Live in Boston. What a great city, and it was a fun eBay Live! Manning the booth with me were Melanie (my best friend from high school, who lives in Boston), her friend Dee, and my mom.

Our hotel was close to the convention center so that we were able to walk there every day of the three-day event. One night, my mom and I even walked down to the Bank of America Pavilion because we heard the band Chicago playing. The concert was about half over, so they let us in for free. It was such a blast! And just because we were walking around.

Talk about walking around, check out this darling piece

BOSTON (ETATS-UNIS), HIER. *Lynn Dralle a publié plusieurs livres de trucs et astuces sur le système eBay.*

Voici la reine des enchères

— SAMEDI 16 JUIN 2007

leParisien

with its figural feet. It turns out that it is from the Walking Ware Big Foot line by Carlton Ware. Carlton Ware was established in 1890 in Stoke-on-Trent England by three men, two of whom eventually left the company. The remaining founder, James Wiltshaw, carried on, but was tragically killed in the Stoke railroad station in 1918. Apparently, he was walking where he should not have been.

His son, Frederick Wiltshaw, was serving in World War I at the time of his father's death, but was allowed a compassionate leave to return home and run his father's company. Being in his early twenties, he had a grasp on what the younger generation wanted. He introduced a competitive lusterware and novelty line and ran the company until his death in 1966. He helped to make Carlton Ware one of the most prolific potteries of all time. To learn more about "prolific," check out story #69 in *Money Making Madness*.

In 1966, the company was sold to Arthur Wood and Sons. By the 1970s, Carlton began producing less elaborate hand-painted items and started concentrating on more modern shapes and patterns. Novelty items like the Walking Ware line became their focus. Due to financial difficulties, production at the pottery was halted in 1992. In 1997, however, the Carlton Ware brand was resurrected by Francis Joseph. It continues to manufacture novelty items today.

This Walking Ware "thing" I sold turned out to be an egg cup. An egg cup is used to serve boiled eggs in their shells. An egg cup is a highly collectible item. There are newsletters, clubs, and conventions for egg cup collecting, which is known as "pocillovy" (from the Latin *"pocillum,"* for "small cup" and "I" for egg). Strange!

Egg cups typically have a round opening to hold the egg and a base to raise the egg and give it stability. These bases are known as "footies." And in my case, they really were footies! And they sold while we were hoofing it all over Boston!

#72 Carved Lion

$20.00
Paid
From: Estate sale

Carved Wood Enkeroll Rampant Lion Vintage Wooden Plaque

Description:
Signed on the back with Enkeroll and a key and quill with ink. Huge 16 by 11". Needs slight cleaning. There are some tiny holes in the wood. A super piece.

Winning Bid: **$152.50**

Ended: 6/16/07
History: 8 bids
Starting Bid: $9.99
Winner: Antioch, CA

Viewed
 000092 X

Carved Lion #72

The Story

We were still in Boston at eBay Live while this was selling. We were invited to a Wiley Publishing Book party to celebrate Marsha Collier's sale of her one-millionth *eBay for Dummies* book. Now that is quite the accomplishment! I had also written a book for Wiley called *The Unofficial Guide to Making Money on eBay,* so we scored an invite.

It was one of the best parties ever! Melanie, my mom, Dee and I got to hang out with Julie and Steve from Wiley. Julie does marketing for the *Dummies* books and Steve is an editor. We also got to spend time with fellow authors Julia Wilkinson and Joel Elad, and had the pleasure of meeting Rich and Cindy Tennant. Rich has done all the cartoons for every single *Dummies* Book. Did you realize that there are over 1,200 *Dummies* books? What an amazing accomplishment. We had a lot of fun. I'm sure all the free wine and sushi didn't hurt our good time! We closed the place down!

So, while we were there, this amazing wood piece sold on eBay. I had paid $20 for it. Despite the fact that I got the company name wrong, it still sold for over $150! I had listed it as an "Enkeroll" piece; when I later discovered that there was a company called "Enkeboll," I emailed and asked what their signature looked like. The signature on my plaque was a key and a plume feather with ink bottle; Paula Hailey from Enkeboll sent me a nice email confirming that my plaque was in fact one of their pieces and explained that "the key and feather stands for Enkeboll (*enk*=ink

boll=circle)." If I had had the correct company name in the auction title would it have sold for more?

Raymond Enkeboll started his company in 1956 in a chicken shed in Venice, California. He began by creating handmade furniture with the care of Old World designers. The company eventually moved from the chicken shed to a space in LA, and then to a larger facility in Carson, California. And I do mean large—75,000 square feet. At this time, the company makes not only Spanish Mediterranean furniture, but also wood embellishments for kitchens, living rooms, and wine cellars. The designs are inspired by folk art and European antiques. Today the company has over 200 employees and produces 550 different items. Wow!

Enkeboll only buys sustainable woods—woods that can be replenished. It uses the finest red oak, hard maple, cherry, white oak, mahogany, black walnut and alder wood. The wood is then carved into pedestal bases, plaques, and corbels (a corbel looks like a triangle or beak and is attached to a wall to support something heavy), often in the figural shapes (like lions!)

Too cool! The lion piece I had must have been vintage to bring in over $150. I was so happy that it sold for so much while we were all dancing the chicken dance at the Wiley party in Boston. I don't remember if we really danced the chicken dance or not. But I bet we did, judging from that photo!

#73 Heubach Vase

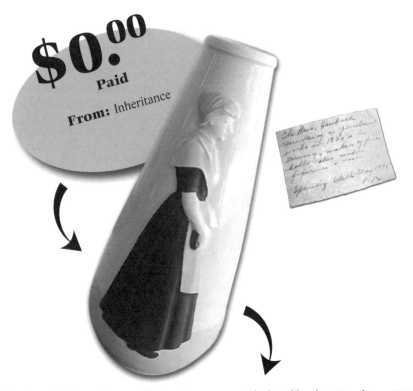

$0.⁰⁰ Paid

From: Inheritance

Heubach Vase Amsterdam Germany Pink Pilgrim Puritan OLD

Description:

This is a great antique vase that was in my grandmother's personal collection. It is unsigned except for an impressed "Amsterdam" on the back lower side. It is 7½" by 3½". It is pink shiny pottery with a matte color base. The woman is dressed in black and looks to be a pilgrim or puritan. If anyone knows anything about it we would appreciate knowing. From my grandmother's note that was tucked inside, she believed it to be Heubach Brothers. In excellent condition.

Winning Bid:

$24.⁹⁹

Ended: 6/27/07
History: 1 bid (sold in store)
Starting Bid: $99.00 then $24.99
Winner: Mexico, MO

Viewed
 X

Heubach Vase #73

The Story

This vase had always been in one of my grandmother's display cabinets—she had twenty of them around her living room. She loved to fill them up with her most beloved antiques, research those pieces, and store the research inside the pieces for future reference.

This vase had one of her notes inside. It was written on pink cardboard, and from the second I touched it, I knew that there was a discount ticket to an antiques show on the other side. My grandma recycled everything. If she got a stack of advertisements to an antique show, she would wait until the show had passed, then cut up the flyers and use them as scrap paper.

This card (which seemed to be from the 1960s judging by the antiques show it advertised) said in her penciled cursive, "The Bros. Heubach Founders of a porcelain works in 1820s in Germany and makers of fine dolls, also made figurines and vases." The note also cited her source for this information: "Spinning Wheel May 1970 p. 12." Back when my grandmother wrote this note, researching an item required serious dedication. I am still so impressed with her work ethic and research skills—no Google then, kids!

Here is some more updated information on Heubach. In 1843, two brothers (Georg and Philipp Heubach) purchased a porcelain factory in Lichten, Germany. It was known as "Gebruder Heubach" (*"Gebruder"* means

"brothers" in German) and from 1840 to 1925 it was best known for its bisque dolls and doll heads. The heads often had molded hair and intaglio eyes, which were created using a technique that gave an illusion of depth and realism. The doll heads were exceptionally well made, with childlike hair styles, dimples on the chins, and expressive faces. Gebruder Heubach also specialized in boy heads—which not many companies did at that time. In 1938, the company went bankrupt.

Gebruder Heubach dolls can be very valuable; I found one that recently sold for $2,600. My grandmother kept two antique Gebruder Heubach baseball players on her mantle for years, but sold them for $295 some time before Houston was born. I just found an identical one on eBay that had sold for $1,300. I wish she would have kept those figurines for Houston!

My grandmother had put a price tag of $150 on this vase (she did that sometimes so that we would know what her personal items were worth), so I tried it at auction for $99. It didn't sell, so I tried it again at $49.99. It still didn't sell. Yikes. I finally listed it in my eBay store at $99. No takers for two years. I lowered the price to $24.99 in 2007, and it finally sold in June.

I wonder why my Grandma thought this piece was Heubach, since Heubach was a German company and this piece was signed "Amsterdam." Well, I will never know. I just wish she hadn't sold the baseball pitcher and batter for less than $300. Ouch, that actually hurts!

#74 My Child Doll Clothes

$3.00/3
Paid
From: Thrift store

Doll Clothes Dress Vintage My Child Playground Outfit

Description:
This doll outfit is still on the original card. Green, orange little sweater, white with brown pockets. Close tape fasteners, hand wash cold water. "My Child" button in a heart. 4" from shoulder to shoulder and 7" from shoulder to hem in length. In great condition. We have a lot of vintage doll dresses and other outfits/sweaters up for sale this week. Most are from the 1980s and 1990s. Some may be handmade.

Winning Bid:

$73.28/3
Ended: 7/7/07
History: 27 bids/3
Starting Bid: $9.99 ea auction
Winner: Australia, Miami, FL

Viewed

000097 X

My Child Doll Clothes   #74

The Story

In July of 2007, something fantastic happened to me with doll clothes! But let me go back to the beginning. I received my Kovels newsletter in the mail about the first week of June. As I was quickly scanning it, I noticed an article on antique doll clothes on the front cover. Fancy 1880s to early 1900s outfits in great condition were selling for over $1,500! I was intrigued.

The next thing I know, I am in my favorite thrift store and the manager walks over and places a huge plastic bin of doll clothes on the counter (literally) right under my nose. Strange, but true! I asked, "How much?" and was told that each dress was $1.

Now, these were not 1900s doll dresses, but 1980s to 1990s larger-sized doll dresses. Most were handmade, but some had manufacturer's tags. I quickly picked out the most pristine of the dresses—28 total.

I got them all listed and couldn't believe all the interest in the "My Child" doll clothes. Someone even emailed me, offering to pay $15 for one of the "My Child" peach-colored dresses if I would end the auction immediately. Bidders occasionally request this; don't do it. Let the auction run its course.

The auctions for these three "My Child" outfits ended on 7-7-7. How lucky is that date? It was lucky for Peter and I, who were on a road trip to celebrate my birthday. Why a road trip? When we attended Book Expo America in New York in May, I had introduced him to one of my editors at Wiley. The editor said to me, "Lynn, you have a book deal, and Peter, you have a conversation." Guess what? My book deal fell through, but Peter got a contract. With his advance, he bought a convertible, and in July we drove it from LA back to Albuquerque. It was a blast!

But let's go back and see why those three doll outfits sold for almost $75! The "My Child" line was made by Mattel from 1985 to 1988. The dolls were adorable, cloth covered, and so soft they seemed to be made of felt. They came in both girl and boy varieties, and featured different hair styles, hair colors, eye colors and even four different skin tones (African American, pale, Hispanic and peach). They were marketed to parents as a doll that you could buy that would look just like your child.

The rarest dolls are the ones with strawberry blonde hair; these were only made in 1988. One sold on eBay recently for $992! The next most valuable dolls are the peach-skinned brunettes and redheads. These are valuable because when Mattel shipped the dolls in cartons of six, only one redhead or one brunette would be included. The rest were blondes.

Hey, I always knew that having strawberry blonde or red hair was rare. But my favorite doll as a child was Dancerina, a blonde ballerina also by Mattel. I tried to replace her recently but found that Dancerinas run about $100 on eBay! I guess I could almost buy her with the profit I made on these doll clothes. I really could have bought her if I had gotten a book deal! Oh, well, just remember to always look for doll clothes and "My Child" dolls!

#75 Tomb of Rachel Plate

$2.00
Paid
From: Thrift store

Brass Plate Tomb of Rachel Israel Tel Aviv City Vintage

Description:
Brass plate is in very good to excellent condition. Says "Tomb of Rachel" and "Made in Israel." Gold floral design. 7½". Neat piece.

Winning Bid:

$25.49
Ended: 7/8/07
History: 7 bids
Starting Bid: $9.99
Winner: Anderson, SC

Viewed
 **X**

Tomb of Rachel Plate   #75

The Story

I had found this plate at a thrift store for $2. It was ironic because that summer, the daughter of my Pilates teacher, Ronnie, was working for me. Ronnie's daughter Rachel was writing up items on my *I Sell* sheets, and when she got to this plate, she said, "How cool!" I told her that if it didn't sell, she could have it. But boy, did it sell!

The Tomb of Rachel is considered the third holiest site in Judaism and has been a destination for prayer and pilgrimage for more than 3,000 years. It is located on the outskirts of Bethlehem, on a site believed to be where Rachel, the wife of Jacob, went into a difficult labor and died giving birth to her son Benjamin. Jacob built a pillar over her grave consisting of a rock with eleven stones on it, one for each of the eleven sons of Jacob who were alive when Rachel died.

Over the centuries, the tomb has changed. A dome was added that was supported by four arches. In 1841, a large two-room building was built. Then, for security reasons, the dome was fortified and enclosed inside a building.

There is a tradition associated with the Tomb of Rachel involving a scarlet thread that is tied around one's neck or wrist. Before the thread may be used, it must be wound around the Tomb of Rachel, which is supposed to transform it into a special charm *("segulah")* which protects the wearer against all forms of danger. It is said to work especially well for pregnant women. You may have seen these worn by Kabbalah believers.

Rachel is considered by many as the "eternal mother" and protector of pregnant women. She cares for the health of loved ones and those in need. She has also become a special symbol of hope for childless women.

My grandmother had a very difficult time having children. It took her four years to get pregnant with my mom. She was very lucky to have been able to give birth to Sharon Lynn, and so am I! I wouldn't be here otherwise. She wasn't so lucky when she tried to have more children. It took another four years for her to get pregnant again. In July of 1940 she gave birth to a son, Marvin Maynard. He lived for one month and finally died from liver complications. It was one of the great tragedies of her life, and something she rarely talked about.

She and my grandfather wanted more children very badly, and my mother wanted siblings. My grandmother wanted to adopt, but back then it wasn't as socially acceptable as it is today and my grandfather objected. It wasn't to be. Maybe she should have made a pilgrimage to the Tomb of Rachel. I know she visited Israel later in her life and was fascinated and enthralled with the country. It just wasn't soon enough.

No wonder this plate sold for $25.49. I am sorry I wasn't able to give it to Ronnie's daughter Rachel, but she understood. I am also very sorry for my grandmother, grandfather, and my mother, for their incredible loss.

#76 Poor Pitiful Pearl

$20.00
Paid

From: Estate sale

Horsman Vintage MIB Poor Pitiful Pearl Doll Perfect WOW

Description:
The "Ugly Betty" doll of the 1950s to 1970s. When do you see one of these mint in the box? Horsman since 1862. She has never been taken out of the box and her hair still has the net in it. Says, "Poor Pitiful Pearl Make her neat! Make her pretty! Love her!" Still has the play booklet in the box. Box is 11" by 20" by 5". The box is tattered with some tape on it etc. Rare find. Check out our auctions for more dolls this week.

Winning Bid:

$82.03

Ended: 7/15/07
History: 22 bids
Starting Bid: $9.99
Winner: Westlake Village, CA

Viewed

000718 X

Poor Pitiful Pearl #76

The Story

When I was little, I couldn't pronounce "Dralle" (which rhymes with "trolley"), so I would tell people that my name was Lynn Dolly. They started calling me "The Dralle Dolly."

I love it when I see vintage (not necessarily even antique) dolls at estate sales. This one came with an outfit that was supposed to transform her from ugly to beautiful. I paid $20 for Poor Pitiful Pearl (or "PPP," as I called her), which I thought was quite a bit, but she was awesome!

She sold on July 15th as we were arriving in Steamboat Springs, Colorado for a week-long baseball tournament. How fun was that? To get to Steamboat Springs is quite the ordeal. We flew from Palm Springs (at 6 am) to Salt Lake City, where we changed to a tiny plane for the rest of our journey. We landed in Hayden, Colorado at about 1 pm, just in time to pick up our SUV and head to the team condo.

The boys had a fantastic week of baseball, and took 13th place! I was so proud of all of them—there were 44 teams participating from around the U.S. It was a really fun week!

But let's get back to the "dolly" and see why she sold for so much. Horsman is the oldest doll company in America, established by Edward Imeson Horsman in 1865. No other company even comes close. Interestingly enough, for the first 40 years, the company didn't manufacture dolls; it imported and distributed German dolls, toys, games, and sporting goods.

In 1905, Horsman finally began to create its own dolls. Most were "composition dolls" which sported wigs or had molded hair and painted eyes. In 1911, the company developed a formula to manufacture what it called "Can't break 'em" dolls. When Edward Horsman died in 1927, the doll company was in trouble. In 1933, a company called Regal dolls took over and revived the company. For a while, dolls were produced under both the Regal and Horsman names, but the company soon realized Horsman was the better brand.

In 1947, after the war, Horsman got into plastic and made vinyl dolls on a very large scale. The company's slogan was "America's Best Known and Best Loved Dolls." In the 1950s, at its peak, Horsman was making 12,000 dolls a day. Horsman made everything in the U.S. Good for them!

The company changed ownership many more times over the years. The competition from Asia in the 1970s was intense, but Horsman stood firm and kept manufacturing its dolls in South Carolina. By 1985, they couldn't compete anymore and they closed their US factory. A wealthy Hong Kong family bought the brand, and Horsman dolls are now produced overseas.

In 1963, Poor Pitiful Pearl was issued. She was either 11½" or 16" tall. Mine was the 16" variety.

Wow, "PPP" was issued the same year as I was. This Dralle "dolly" got lucky when Pearl sold for more than four times what I paid for her. That investment helped pay for some of that fun baseball trip!

#77 Celadon Chop Plate

$1.00 Paid
From: Garage sale

Celadon Chop Plate Asian Charger Serving Platter Green

Description:
This beautiful piece is 13" and in great condition. No chip, no cracks, but some crazing. No signatures. I can't tell the age of this piece. But it is really neat.

Winning Bid:

$52.51
Ended: 8/6/07
History: 8 bids
Starting Bid: $9.99 each
Winners: Dallas, TX

Viewed

000110 X

Celadon Chop Plate #77

The Story

Celadon green pottery typically sells well. "Celadon" is a term used for ceramics with a particular type of glaze and also a specific color. It was invented in ancient China in the Zhejiang Province (often abbreviated to "Zhe"), which is on China's east coast. The color is generally a pale jade green and it is lovely.

It is strange, but I have been to China once—but very briefly. When my grandmother took my brother Lee and I to Hong Kong in the late 1970s, we took a one-day trip into China. All I can remember is that there were tons of bicycles and that the only thing to drink was warm orange Fanta. Isn't it weird what you remember from your youth and trips? Memories ... I may start singing...and nobody wants that.

There seem to be a lot of theories about the origin of the word "celadon." It may come from European collectors of celadon ware, who borrowed the word from a popular French novel called *L'Astree* which featured a character named Celadon. Celadon was a shepherd who always dressed in pale green ribbons.

Another theory is that "celadon" comes from the name "Saladin," the Sultan of Ayyubid, who is supposed to have sent forty pieces of celadon-like pottery to the Sultan of Syria in the 1100s.

The third suggestion is that the word comes from the Sanskrit words *"sila dhara." "Sila"* means "stone" and *"dhara"* means "green." Many of the sacred texts of Buddhism and Hinduism are written in Sanskrit, which is one of the 22 official languages of India. Wow! How can a country have 22 languages? And, could it be even more strange that my favorite number is 22?

Celadon glaze is a transparent crackle that comes in a wide variety of colors: white, grey, blue, and yellow. The most famous celadon color range, however, goes from a very pale green crackle to a deep intense green, often mimicking the green shades of jade. The color is made by putting iron oxide in the glaze recipe.

Whatever the history of the name and the glaze recipe, celadon ware is very beautiful, and once you see it, you will remember it.

This was selling as the Queen's Court inner circle was just starting. I can't believe that we have been doing the Queen's Court for so long. It has been extremely successful, and so much fun for all of us involved. The Queen's Court is a private community where members exchange stories, and I (and other members) help evaluate each others' hard-to-identify items. We also have monthly teleseminars and an extra monthly gift. It has added a lot of joy to my life. Thank you, Queen's Court members!

And thank you, Grandma, for teaching me what celadon is. My $1 plate sold for over $50! Celadon is always a great seller, and the Queen's Court members are an amazing group! I am blessed.

#78 Red Wooden Dolls Chair

$4.00
Paid
From: Estate sale

Antique Vintage Childs Dolls Chair Red Wood Folk Art

Description:
19" by 8" by 9". A chair for a doll or a very, very small child. I would guess it is antique. Hand painted and very folk art. 1920s to 1940s. In good condition with some nicks and dings. Darling!

Winning Bid: **$46.00**

Ended: 8/7/07
History: 4 bids
Starting Bid: $9.99
Winner: Ohio

Viewed
 X

Red Wooden Dolls Chair   #78

The Story

This sold on the Sunday that we were shooting the first video (oops, I mean DVD) for *The Queen's Academy*. It was about how to ship, so it was very appropriate that we sold this large, tricky-to-ship item during filming! The DVD shooting day was so much fun. Jason, Carmen's husband, filmed me, Mo, and Carmen shipping from our eBay room and teaching in my dining room.

There are even great outtakes of Mo and Carmen popping out of a huge shipping box—or so I'm told, since I never watch any of my own DVDs. It is too painful!

We charged $19.95 for shipping/handling/insurance—also known as s/h/i—to send this chair via UPS to Ohio. It ended up costing us $11.07, plus about $4 in packing supplies (big box, bubble wrap, and packing peanuts); the other $5 went towards paying my shipping assistant (aka Carmen).

I think this little chair sold for almost $50 because it was decorated in a folk art style. It was hand painted and had a darling shield on the seat with flowers painted inside of it. The term "folk art" is typically applied to functional pieces made by people who have had little or no formal schooling in art. The styles and content are usually handed down through generations.

The chair may also have been bought to display antique dolls. Doll collectors are an interesting bunch who take their displays very seriously. Aaron Spelling's widow Candy Spelling had an entire room in her home ("The Manor," with 56,000 square feet) dedicated to her doll collection.

I just watched a video about it, and it was kind of creepy.

Speaking of creepy and dolls, we have a little leprechaun doll in the house that moves around. We sold him once, but when we went to find him, he was not in his box. We had to refund the buyer's money, and then the doll showed up weeks later in a totally different place. I came home one weekend after a baseball tournament to find that my entire living room had been cleaned, and sitting on my marble table was the leprechaun. Did he clean all the eBay items out of my living room, or did Carmen?

After a Queen's Court call the other night, Carmen made me hide the leprechaun in Mo's car. Mo almost had a heart attack when she found him. The leprechaun is now sitting on my desk because Mo wants me to hide him in Carmen's purse.

As I was writing this story, I suddenly heard a creepy voice say, "Mommy, can you make me dinner?" There was no one in my office. I thought, "Oh, my goodness, the leprechaun is talking!" Then I saw Mo peeking through my office door. She said I looked like I had seen a ghost. Thanks, Mo!

As you can tell, we have a lot of fun around here—just as we had fun making the shipping DVD. If you haven't seen it, I highly recommend it—educational and good for a laugh. And while we were making it, we sold this darling chair for a lot of money! And we now have a leprechaun tradition that will be around for a long time, I'm afraid—kind of like folk art! I think the leprechaun may even show up at Live Boot Camp this year.

#79 Dreamie Gund Bunny

$3.00
Paid
From: Estate sale

Dreamie Gund J Swedlin Bunny Rabbit Toy Doll Vintage

Description:
Really neat Eames-era stuffed animal toy. Has tags. 19" by 8" and quite large. In very good to excellent condition. A Gund product. J. Swedlin Inc. 200 5th Avenue New York New York.

Winning Bid:

$52.89

Ended: 8/15/07
History: 3 bids
Starting Bid: $9.99
Winner: Centennial, Colorado

Viewed

000071 X

Dreamie Gund Bunny #79

The Story

I got this for $3 at an estate sale. I took photos of it before we went to Bellingham for the summer so I could list it from my mom's beach house. It was a really cute vintage Gund bunny rabbit that still had the tags. I remembered that Saul (one of my original Boot Campers) had bought a stuffed animal at a garage sale in Palm Springs and it sold for a lot.

The Dreamie line of toys, which had a cat and a rabbit, was made popular by Gund in the 1940s. This rabbit was style 232/10 and was issued in 1942, when my dad was eight years old and my mom six. The original selling price was $1.98. Crazy that this many years later, the tag was still on this rabbit. No wonder it sold for so much.

Gund has been making teddy bears and other soft toys since 1898. Gund was founded in Norwalk, Connecticut by a German immigrant named Adolph Gund. Adolph ran the company until 1925, when he retired and sold the business to a young Russian immigrant, Jacob Swedlin, who had worked for him since 1907. They made an agreement that the company's name would always remain Gund. Adolph Gund never had any children, so perhaps this was his way of making sure his name carried on.

In 1969, control of Gund went to Swedlin's daughter Rita and her husband Herbert Raiffe, and then passed to their son Bruce in 1993.

The Gund company was a pioneer in the toy industry. It set safety standards, invented key manufacturing processes, and (after Joseph Swedlin bought the company) started the practice of licensing well-known characters. Gund had deals with Felix the Cat, Mickey Mouse, and Popeye.

The company is now based in Edison, New Jersey and is known worldwide for its top-quality useable play toys and also its collectibles. The company's motto is "Gotta Getta Gund, The World's Most Huggable...since 1898."

Lola, who bought this darling rabbit from me on eBay, sent me this email:

> I love my bunny! I have been collecting vintage stuffed rabbits for ten years. I grew up being taken care of by my grandmothers and saw pictures of all of their toys. None of those survived, but I wanted toys that looked like theirs, not the new ones that my friends had. I like the fact that they have some miles on them and have a story to tell.
>
> My collection consists of Steiff, Rushton, Gund, Shuco and some with no labels. Right now I own 51 rabbits (I am a bit picky) and have found it quite difficult to find any new ones. My husband says it is because I have them all already The one I purchased from you is one of my biggest (and one of my favorites)! Thanks!

Lola had a fantastic set of grandmas who helped raise her. I totally understand why she collects these darling rabbits. Thanks for sharing your collection with us. P.S. My name in high school Spanish class was Lola. Gotta love it! Gotta Getta Gund!

#80 Red Le Creuset Skillet

$1.00 Paid

From: Garage sale in Bellingham, WA

Le Creuset Griddle Pan Skillet France Red Vintage Help

Description:
This is signed "Made in France" with a round indented circle. I think that this is the signature for Le Creuset but I couldn't find a sample anywhere on the Internet. Please let me know if you know. This is a great enamel piece of cookware. Black base and grey interior. 12½" by 8½" by 14" to the handle. Rounded rectangle. Needs slight cleaning and has some wear.

Winning Bid:

$46.00

Ended: 8/18/07
History: 13
Starting Bid: $9.99
Winners: Oak Park, IL

Viewed
 X

Red Le Creuset Skillet #80

The Story

I was at a garage sale in Bellingham when I saw this filthy pan. We try to spend at least three weeks in Bellingham every summer. I turned over this dirty orange (or so I thought) enamel pan—and was very pleased to see that it was signed "France." How much? I asked. Only $1. Sold!

When I got back to my mom's beach house I showed it to her (with her master's degree in home economics, as you all know). She said, "Let me show you how to clean that." I usually never clean ANYTHING. But I am pleased to report that I let her clean this piece because it was disgustingly filthy.

She sprayed it all over with regular oven cleaner, waited about twenty minutes, and you won't believe how well it turned out! It was a red pan—not orange—even better!

Then she suggested that the beach rocks in front of her cabin would make a great background for a photo. Amazing how neat this pan looked on the rocks. I felt like I was taking a picture for a Pottery Barn or Williams Sonoma catalog. I think I may have made it look too good!

I started doing some research. I had a hunch that the pan was Le Creuset, but when I've had those pieces in the past, they were usually clearly marked. I couldn't find a photo of a signature like this one, so I put it on eBay with this disclaimer: "This is signed 'Made in France' with a round indented circle. I think that this is the signature for Le Creuset, but I couldn't find a sample anywhere on the Internet. Please let me know if you know!"

Within a few hours, a nice eBayer sent me this info: "This is probably a piece made by the company Cousances, which was, like Le Creuset, based in France. At that time they were making cast iron similar to Le Creuset and Le Creuset eventually bought them out."

Le Creuset is cast iron cookware with an enamel finish—it is what you see on many of the cooking shows. It has the heating properties of iron with the stain-resistant finish of enamel.

Other manufacturers of high-end enameled cast iron are Copco and Descoware (which was also purchased by Le Creuset—see story #22). Le Creuset bought Cousances in the 1960s, but there are still people who prefer Cousances pieces and will seek them out second-hand. These older pieces sell well on eBay.

When buying enameled cast iron to sell on eBay, check for chips in the enamel and signs of wear. Perfect pieces sell for the most. As you've already seen, even pieces which are quite dirty will clean up nicely.

This sold on my Mom's birthday, and once again we had a theme party. This time it was 1960s to 1970s—right when my neat pan was made. Check us out. Gotta love Houston in that white suit! Gotta buy European enamel cookware when you see it!

#81 Mideke Vase

25¢ Paid

From: Garage sale in Bellingham, WA

B400 Mideke

Louis Mideke Hand Signed Vintage Blue Vase Test Glaze

Description:

I think this may be a Mideke glaze test piece because of the number on the base. I found this little gem at an estate sale in Bellingham. It is darling and is a blue glaze with crackles. The base is uneven. Most of the Mideke pieces I have seen are earthtones. 3½" by 2¾" and in excellent condition. I believe that this dates to the 1960s because of the hand signature instead of a stamp.

Winning Bid:

$81.⁰⁰

Ended: 8/18/07
History: 7 bids
Starting Bid: $9.99
Winner: Glen Ridge, NJ

Viewed

000995 X

Mideke Vase #81

The Story

I was still in Bellingham with H & I (not handling and insurance—Houston and Indy), and I had 300 *I Sell* sheets ready to be listed and staring me in the face. So I didn't really need to go out to yard sales and I didn't really feel like going, but of course we went anyway.

The first sale we hit was five houses down from my mom's old house. The driveway was so steep that we barely made it up to the top. The ladies holding the sale were having a lot of fun. I filled up a huge box with stuff and was told it only added up to $19.75. I gave one of the ladies a $20 bill and said, "Don't give me any change; let me find a 25-cent item." You won't believe what I picked up next.

It was a little blue vase, signed on the base with "Mideke." The lady having the sale said, "Sure, that can be a quarter!" Score!

Louis Mideke was a Bellingham potter, and my grandmother and I had bought all the pottery remaining from the Mideke estate in 1993. We sold the 300-plus items in my grandmother's antiques store over the years.

I got an email from an old family friend when I listed this item and I posted this on my auction. "I knew Louis Mideke and his wife; he was quite a guy and an excellent potter. I remember seeing all his little jars of 'test' glazes. Never saw the blue crackle. I suspect it was one of his tests."

Robin Reynolds, another friend of the Midekes, told me that when Louis would test a glaze he sometimes put a number on the base so he would know the recipe.

Mideke made his pot-

tery and other artwork in a chicken coop behind his house on Sunset Drive. My grandma was a friend and a huge fan, and she visited him often to purchase his art. Louis was a character, just like my grandmother. When Mideke was named a "Living Treasure" by the Bellingham Municipal Arts Commission, he was described as being "like a good loaf of sourdough bread; crusty on top and soft as a marshmallow inside...leavened by many years of hard work and mellowed by the gentleness of his temperament and soul." My grandma always said that she was tough on the outside but as soft as a marshmallow on the inside, and it was true!

Louis passed away in 1989, after making close to 100,000 pieces. His son Michael said that, "Early in his career Louis entered pieces in shows and won some honors, but this aspect of the 'art' business did not appeal to him. He felt pottery should be useful, beautiful to see and touch, and accessible to the people. He was self-educated."

Mideke did experiment with his art, and one result was this little test piece which ended up selling for $81 (324 times what I paid for it) and was sent to New Jersey. Louis' pieces are exhibited in the Smithsonian, and now we know that he has fans all over the world.

#82 Wade Figurines

$0.⁰⁰
Paid
From: Garage sale in Bellingham, WA

Huge Lot 88 Wade Rose Tea Animals Noahs Ark Circus ETC

Description:
These are all signed "Wade England" and came in Rose Tea boxes. They are in very good to excellent condition. About 4 of them have slight nicks. There are 17 from the Noah's Ark series, 11 from the circus collection and 60 from the endangered species collection. Known as Wade Whimsies. Vintage and neat.

Winning Bid:

$49.⁰⁰
Ended: 8/18/07
History: 11 bids
Starting Bid: $9.99
Winners: Kent, OH

Viewed

000197 X

The Story

As I was leaving that garage sale by my mom's old house where I got the Mideke vase for 25 cents, I noticed a box of Wade figurines on the ground. I used to collect them and I asked, "How much?" The seller replied, "Oh, those are in the free pile." Score!

When I was little and went with my grandmother to antique shows, she wanted me to collect things so that I would have fun going on "the hunt" with her. One of the things that I collected were the Wade figurines.

I remember one big antiques show that was held in Portland, Oregon every summer. On Sunday there would be a huge flea market in the same building as the antiques show. Most of the dealers—including my grandma and I—would wait in line for the big doors to open, and when they did we would rush inside. That summer, she had given me $5 to spend, and I was on "the hunt" for Whimsies.

It is funny how clearly I remember that day and the excitement of "the hunt." I guess that is why eBay is still such a blast for me. I still experience the thrill of finding treasures and then the gratification of making a quick profit. I was only about eleven years old on that day in Portland, and I found ten of the little figurines for 50 cents each. I specifically remember getting the white poodle, and you know, I still have that collection in a box somewhere. Now that is scary!

It was strange being at a sale so close to my mom's old house. My mom's house had a super steep driveway, and I can still remember Lee and I trying to push my grandmother's wheelchair to the front door one Christmas when it was snowy and icy. We were all laughing, but it was kind of scary because she could have gotten hurt. But everything was an adventure to my grandmother, and we got her to the top with no problem.

The Wade family founded Wade Ceramics in 1810 in Stoke on Trent England. It is still in business today, manufacturing primarily liquor containers. In 1953, Sir George Wade (who called himself "The Jolly Potter") developed the Whimsies. The Jolly Potter was quite the character. He was a very shrewd businessman and was loved by family, friends, and army buddies alike. He was a business genius but was controversial because of his politics and love of the ladies. He passed away in 1986 at the age of 97.

The Whimsies, which he created, were small solid ceramic animals. They were sold in retail stores and beginning in 1960 were also given away with Red Rose tea. The Whimsies are quite collectible and were released in several different series. It was these Whimsies that made Wade a household name here in America.

I had 88 of these Whimsies and decided to sell them all in one big lot. I didn't want to mess around with breaking them out into different smaller lots. They usually sell for about $1 each in large lots, but my lot went for only $49. Boo hoo! Just kidding. What a great return on a FREE item!

#83 Donna RuBert Jasmine Doll

$10.00
Paid

From: Garage sale in Bellingham, WA

Donna RuBert Doll #143 LE Bisque Butterfly CUTE

Description:
32" doll. I need help with the name if anyone knows. Signed "Donna RuBert" and this doll has a very low number, #143 out of only 1000 made. Circa 2000. So lifelike. This doll has rasta braids with beads. Could be an island girl. Yellow dress and sweater with a hat with a butterfly on it. She is also holding a container with a butterfly in it. Looks to be in perfect condition.

Winning Bid:

$102.00

Ended: 8/18/07
History: 11 bids
Starting Bid: $24.99
Winner: Naples, FL

Viewed

000114 X

Donna RuBert Jasmine Doll #83

The Story

We were out garage saling by my rental house on Nevada Street. The streets all go in alphabetical order, which makes it pretty easy to find your way around. There is Lakeway, then Moore, Nevada, Orleans, Puget, Queen, Racine, Toledo, Undine, and so on. I can't believe I just did that from memory! Two of my best friends from high school, Kathy Rutan and Mindy Maier, lived off of Toledo.

I feel comfortable garage saling in this area because I spent a lot of time in my green Volkswagen bug on these hills. However, the garage sale that my mom and I stopped at on Orleans was a little creepy. It was in a barn-type garage behind the house and there were toys and dolls all over, set up like they were alive.

I bought two of these Donna RuBert dolls for $10 each. They were huge—almost life-size—and very realistic. They actually scared me. My mom didn't go into the sale with me, so when I walked out carrying these two huge babies, it freaked her out!

Donna Ru-Bert was a born artist. She quit college in her sophomore year to travel the world and study with famous art-

ists. She started out as a painter and portrait sculptor, and by her twenties had such a large following that she was awarded a lifetime teaching certificate for California colleges. Amazing! She taught her realistic method of painting and drawing for eighteen years.

Even with all this success, Donna felt that something was missing. In 1990, she tried combining her painting with sculpting, and "June," her first doll, was born. She loves making dolls and it shows. Can you believe how realistic these two dolls are?

Donna soon became a partner in the Doll Artworks company and within a year this mold-making doll company became one of the largest and most recognized in the world. Donna's dolls sell out quickly on many home shopping networks like HSN, Home Shopping Europe, and Shopping Channel (HSE). Good for her!

Donna's daughter Kelly is also a famous doll artist, and they are both Doty winners. A Doty is one of the most prestigious awards in the doll world. Most of Donna's and Kelly's dolls are numbered limited editions, which adds to their collectibility.

I couldn't find the names of my two dolls before I listed them, but a nice eBayer did email me later to let me know that this one's name was Jasmine. I took the photos on my mom's Adirondack beach chair on her deck. Boy—these dolls looked even more lifelike on that chair. Jasmine ended up selling for over $100, and the other RuBert doll sold about one and a half years later out of my eBay store for $69.99. Not bad for a $20 investment!

#84 Victorian Embroidered Picture

$0.⁰⁰ Paid

From: Inheritance

Antique Picture Frame Victorian Paddi Hals Embroidery

Description:
Neat piece is 10" by 9". Has cracks and nicks. I would guess 1880s to 1900s. Says "Paddi Hals" and "31/11." Needs cleaning. Floral flower basket is hand stitched. Classic and shabby chic.

Winning Bid:

$37.⁰⁰

Ended: 8/18/07
History: 7 bids
Starting Bid: $9.99
Winner: New York, NY

Viewed
 X

Victorian Embroidered Picture #84

The Story

I inherited this from my grand-mother's antique shop. It was one of those things that I thought I would never get around to listing because quite honestly, I didn't think it would sell for $9.99. Luckily, I was wrong!

As this was selling, I was sitting at my computer in my mom's beach house looking out the window at the wonderful sunny day and taking a test. I thought my days of test-taking were long past. But no, I had decided to try to become an eBay Certified Service Provider. eBay certifies certain companies and individuals after putting them through a rigorous examination process. They speak to ten of your customers, look at all of your teaching tools, and then ask you to take an actual examination that you have to re-take every year! There are only about 35 Certified Service Providers, so it is a very prestigious honor.

I had to pass this test. It was 90 minutes long and some of the questions were seriously very difficult. I needed to get 80% or more correct or I would have to take it again. As I finished the test, I thought I had just eked out 80%, but no—the final screen read 79% correct! I was crushed. But one of the questions had been a little ambiguous.

It asked if you could sell an item for a charity without first signing up through Mission Fish. I said "yes" because you can always choose to donate 100% of an auction to a particular charity. The correct answer was "no," because in order to be a recognized charity, that charity must sign up through Mission Fish. I emailed eBay Certified Provider liaison, Laura Della Torre, to explain my answer and the next thing you know...I was an eBay Certified Service Provider. Too cool!

The only problem is that now every summer, I have to retake the same very difficult exam. At least this awesome Victorian piece was selling for a lot of money while I was slaving away.

Talk about slaving away. In Victorian times, it was hard for women to find items to decorate their homes. The reason for this may have been due to financial constraints, or maybe just because they didn't have the shopping options then that we have today—malls, the Internet, specialty stores, catalogs, and so on.

So, many ladies of that era turned to crafts. They produced beautiful and useful decorations for themselves, their families, their friends, and their homes. They often recycled items and made them into beautiful pieces of art to adorn their living spaces.

I think that this piece was darling. It had a flower basket and lovely flowers on it. It also said "Paddi Hals," but for the life of me I couldn't find out what that means. Oh, well, Victorian hand-crafts can sell for big bucks on eBay. Keep your eyes open for pincushions, tablecloths, pictures, pillows and anything else made by hand in the 1880s. Remember that corn-shaped pincushion mentioned in my ezine that a reader sold for several thousand dollars? I just need to find one of those!

#85 Shawnee Corn Cream & Sugar

$20.⁰⁰/2
Paid
From: Estate sale

Shawnee USA Covered Corn Maize Sugar Bowl Pottery CUTE
Shawnee USA Creamer Pitcher Corn Cob Maize Pottery CUTE

Description:

This covered sugar bowl is signed "USA" and measures 5¾" by 5". In very good to excellent condition with no chips, no cracks, no crazing. We have the creamer up for sale in a separate auction.

This creamer is 5" by 5". There is a small chip on the inside of the lip but the glaze goes over part of it so it could have been done in the making. No other chips or cracks. We have the matching sugar bowl up for sale in a separate auction.

Winning Bid: $146.⁴³/2

Ended: 8/24/07
History: 20 bids/2
Starting Bid: $9.99 ea
Winner: Simi Valley, CA

Viewed
 **X**

Shawnee Corn Cream & Sugar #85

The Story

When I was about twelve years old I decided to collect Shawnee pottery. My grandmother always sold reference books in her store and at antique shows. She said that whenever you acquire a new piece, you should also acquire a book to go with it because reference books were invaluable. She was right, again!

When I would accompany her to antiques shows, I would help set up the white cardboard display cases that held those books. At one show, a book on Shawnee pottery caught my eye. I mentioned to my grandmother that it looked interesting and of course she gave it to me right on the spot. I was fascinated by the history of the company and immediately began looking for pottery pieces that were signed with an incised "USA."

The reason for this simple signature is that many of the Shawnee Pottery pieces left the factory with paper labels or stickers showing their logo. Over the years, many of these labels were removed or fell off, leaving only the incised marking. Other Shawnee signatures to look for besides just "USA" are "Patented Mugsey USA," "Patented Winnie USA," "USA 6," and any signature that says "Shawnee."

Shawnee gets its name and distinctive mark from a Shawnee arrowhead found on the Zanesville, Ohio, site where the plant was founded in 1937. That was a good time to start an American pottery factory. It was when the first "Buy American" campaigns were getting started and U.S. resentment of the dominance of Asian and European goods was growing. Shawnee was perfectly poised to offer dinnerware and pottery to the U.S. market.

Shawnee pottery was originally mass-produced to be sold in dime stores such as Woolworth, McCrory, and S.S. Kresge. Many of these stores actually supplied designs to the Shawnee company with the understanding that they would purchase the items after they were made. If you can believe it, many of the early pieces retailed for between ten and thirty cents!

The best known Shawnee kitchenware is probably the Corn line, which began as a Proctor and Gamble "premium." Premiums were basically giveaways; customers mailed in a certain number of labels and in return received a free piece of kitchenware. The Shawnee premium line was originally known as "White Corn" because the corn in the pattern was white. In 1946, the corn was changed to yellow, and the updated pattern was called "Corn King." In 1954, Shawnee changed the color for the last time to a lighter yellow, darkened the green leaves, and called the pattern "Corn Queen."

I couldn't believe that this creamer and sugar in the Corn line sold for $146.43! I was blown away, and wished that I had continued collecting Shawnee. I only ever had a few pieces, but some Shawnee items can sell in the $1,000 range! I am wondering if my pattern was Corn King or Queen. It had to be Queen, since I am the Queen of Auctions—and quite possibly the Queen of Corny.

#86 Broken Doll Head

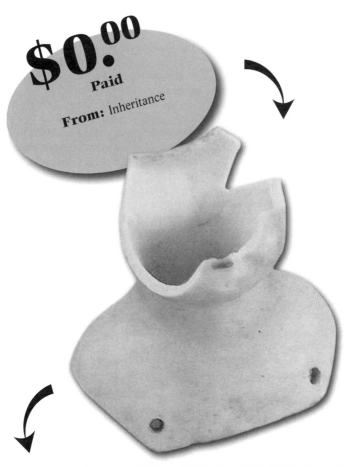

$0.⁰⁰

Paid

From: Inheritance

Bisque Broken Doll Head Marked II 1900 Fun Signature

Description:
Bisque doll head is broken. Antique and very "as is." Just fun to have as a signature piece example, or it may be repairable with a lot of imagination. 2¾" by 1¾" by 2¼". Head #4621.

Winning Bid:

$9.⁹⁹

Ended: 8/30/07
History: 1 bid (sold in store)
Starting Bid: $9.99
Winner: MI

Viewed

000278 X

Broken Doll Head #86

The Story

As many of you know, my grandmother never threw anything away that she thought could be recycled or used as an example. This broken doll head was sure one of those items. When I pulled it out of one of the boxes I had inherited, I had to laugh at its $2.50 price tag and our gall in thinking anyone would pay that much for it.

I figured, "Why not try it on eBay?" Stranger things have sold. We listed it in 2005, but there were no takers. It then sat in my eBay store until 2007, when it finally found a buyer. Two years is as long as I'll keep an item in my eBay store, and this doll head barely made it. But it did finally sell!

Bisque dolls came into fashion in the late 1860s. Before then, dolls were made of glazed porcelain. Using bisque allowed doll makers to create more realistic-looking dolls because they could control skin tone. These antique dolls usually had bisque heads, arms, and feet, with leather or cloth bodies. In later years, the bodies were made of "composition," which is a mixture of wood pulp, sawdust, and glue. Antique unglazed bisque dolls are very collectible and are usually signed on the back of the neck or on the shoulder.

I think my grandmother collected dolls and doll parts over the years because she inherited her mother's bisque doll after her mother died. That doll was about the only thing my grandmother had to remember her mother by as she grew up. I am sure that having her mother's doll gave my grandma some comfort.

My grandmother's stepmother, Elsie, had a baby boy in 1919. His name was William George Sussex and they called him Billie. My grandmother loved Billie, and so did everyone else. He was a wonderful child. At age ten, Billie got a boil on his arm. A boil is caused when a hair turns inward and the sore gets infected.

Back in 1929, they didn't think boils were a big deal, so they didn't take him to the hospital to have it lanced. Billie passed away because of that boil and my grandmother never got over losing her little brother. She was seventeen years old when that happened. Luckily, two years later, my grandmother's dad and stepmother had another boy, George Robert Sussex.

My grandma always kept a photo of Billie on her mantle. It was taken right before he died; he is out playing in a huge pile of snow. My grandmother also kept his Bible in one of her display cases. She gave me that photo and Billie's little Bible before she died.

As Peter said to me, "Sometimes when you sell things on eBay you are not just making money; you're providing a valuable service by helping someone find something that is very important to them." Maybe this broken bisque doll head has now been repaired and made into a doll that means more to the new owner than we will ever know.

#87 New Wave Band Buttons

$40.00/117
Paid
From: Ex-husband

1980's Pin Vintage Punk Devo Guy Screaming Red Black

Description:
1¼" pin or button. Black outline of a guy screaming. Red and white. We have a lot of these vintage buttons pins up for sale this week. I bought a collection that was accumulated in Europe and the U.S. in the 1980s. New Wave and some punk. Check out all our auctions for some really great 80s bands and some really obscure ones!

Winning Bid: **$614.75/117**

Ended: 9/10/07 to present
History: 121 bids/117 (auction & store)
Starting Bid: $4.99 ea
Winners: GA, CA, UK, OH, WA, PA, Italy, Germany

Viewed
 X

New Wave Band Buttons #87

The Story

My ex-husband, William, lived in England in 1984 for a semester with the University of Oregon. Strangely enough, I was also in Europe, but living in Spain at that exact same time doing a semester with USC. We didn't know each other.

William was really into music, so he saw a lot of concerts and bought a lot of these buttons. He just told me that the old concert tickets included in the box of stuff I bought from him will also sell on eBay. I will have to go and find that box—although it may take me three weeks, because who knows where it is?

He also just in-formed me that the real reason he did the semester abroad was not to study, but to go to concerts, buy "badges," and collect T-shirts. I am sure his mother would appreciate having this in-formation. I had sev-eral reasons for doing my semester abroad. I wanted to minor in Spanish, I wanted to take a speech class

with only one student in it (me!), and I wanted to travel around Europe.

The most upsetting part of the in-formation I just learned is not the fact that my ex-husband wasn't serious about school—I already knew that—but the fact that I called these items "pins" and "buttons," when in Eng-land, they are known as "badges." Darn it! If I would have used the cor-rect term, they probably would have sold for more.

In any event, I bought 125 BADG-ES from William for $40 and decided

to list them all separately starting at $4.99. I don't typically do this (I never list anything for less than $9.99, be-cause it's just not worth my time), but I knew I would be happy getting $5 for each of them. I waited until eBay was having a listing sale and got all 125 auctions entered. I ended up paying $43.75 in listing fees.

It was a LOT of work for me to list these all separately, so I seriously de-served a large profit margin. To date, we have sold 117 of these badges, leav-ing only eight in my eBay store. Most sold at $4.99 out of the store, but some did sell for slightly higher prices at auction. Altogether, the badges that sold brought in $614.75!

Don't overlook any type of pin, button, or "badge." Look for vintage and antique political or campaign buttons. A campaign pin from 1908 (which said, "Enemies of Special Privilege") sold recently for $1,005. A Disney cast member vintage security badge sold for $330. Also, keep your eye out for school pins. A "Stanford School of Nursing" pin from 1947 recently sold for $426.

None of my pins sold for more than $9.99, but doing the listings for these great New Wave and punk 1980s bands such as David Bowie, Associ-ates, Johnny Rotten, REM, Adam & the Ants, Duran Duran, English Beat, Devo, and Simple Minds brought back a lot of fun memories! And I made money. Nothing better than that.

#88 Murano Glass Kiwi

$20.00 Paid

From: Estate sale

Murano Italian Art Glass Kiwi Bird Green RARE Huge NEAT

Description:
This is a very large and heavy piece of Italian art glass. Beautiful shades of green and looks vintage also. 6" by 8¼" by 5½". Very heavy and high quality.

Winning Bid:

$51.00

Ended: 9/21/07
History: 4 bids
Starting Bid: $24.99
Winner: Newport Beach, CA

Viewed
 **X**

Murano Glass Kiwi #88

The Story

Every Live Boot Camp gets a mascot, and the La Quinta 2007 event was no exception. I had bought this darling kiwi at an estate sale for $20. I love Italian art glass and knew that I couldn't lose. I was going to start her at $24.99 just to be sure.

The kiwi became our mascot. I am holding her in the photo that shows everyone running towards the camera. Too funny. I had my mom write up the auction during Boot Camp and I listed it a few days after camp ended. For once, our mascot sold. I still have a creepy duck in my office from LA Boot Camp that never did sell!

The kiwi is the official bird of New Zealand. It is shy and usually nocturnal. Kiwis' nostrils are at the ends of their long beaks, so they have a highly developed sense of smell, which is unusual in birds. The male and female kiwi are monogamous and live their entire lives as a couple. These relationships can last for up to twenty years. Pretty cool!

We had seventeen students at the La Quinta Boot Camp and it was a blast. We went to a "private screening" at a local thrift store, hit tons of great garage sales, had a fun dinner out at the Crab Shack in La Quinta, and learned a bunch!

Murano glass comes from the Venetian island of (you guessed it) Murano. Murano was a commercial port starting in the seventh century. Murano glassmaking began in 1291 when the Venetian rulers ordered their glassmakers to move their factories to the island. They did this because they were concerned about the risk of fire from the glassmakers' furnaces destroying Venice's (wooden) buildings.

The glassmakers on Murano became wealthy and prominent. By the 1300s, they had been granted immunity from prosecution and their daughters had married into the most affluent families. Despite—or maybe because of—their importance, the glassmakers were not allowed to leave the Venetian republic (a "republic" is a country not governed by a hereditary monarch such as a king or queen). Strange.

The glassmakers of Murano have invented many different kinds of glassmaking techniques over the centuries: enameled glass *("smalto"),* glass with threads *("aventurine"),* thousand flowers glass *("millefiori"),* and even milk glass *("lattimo").* Some of the more famous glassmakers from Murano are Venini, Barovier & Toso, Seguso, and Pauly.

Most of the Murano art glass I've sold has not been signed—I just get a feeling when I pick up a really well-made piece of glass that it is from Italy. Murano glassmakers tended to produce a lot of animals and birds, so I was pretty confident that this was a Murano piece. I have never been questioned by a buyer for calling something Venetian or Murano, and that, as they say, is a "good thing."

Another good thing is that once you have attended a Live Boot Camp, you are a friend for life, to me, Carmen, Mo, Lee, my mom, and my kids. We will not allow you to leave our republic—although maybe it is a monarchy, because I am a "Queen"!

#89 Shawnee Dutch Cookie Jar

$18.00
Paid
From: Garage sale

Shawnee Gold Dutch Girl Cookie Jar USA Vintage RARE WOW

Description:
Cookie jar is 7⅞" by 12". Chip at rim in the top inside of base inside her skirt. You can barely see it and it is a flake chip. Says "Cooky" on her shoulder. Otherwise in good condition. Signed "USA." Skirt has flowers but no tulip. Some wear to gold trim.

Winning Bid:

$47.00

Ended: 9/21/07
History: 5 bids
Starting Bid: $24.99
Winner: Iowa

Viewed
 X

Shawnee Dutch Cookie Jar #89

The Story

I had been approached by a company out of Florida to film an infomercial about how to sell on eBay. The infomercial team came out and shot at my Live Boot Camp and then I flew to Tampa to shoot the in-studio portion. It was a blast!

I hand-carried this cookie jar with me on the plane to feature it in the show. It was still up for sale while we were filming, and one of my ezine readers ended up buying her. Deb said, "I bought her because I have a weakness for Shawnee pottery as well as a Dutch heritage. I've enjoyed her a lot!" All quite strange and surreal.

But let's get back to the Shawnee history that we talked about in story #85.

Shawnee is well-known for salt and pepper shakers, wall pockets, baking dishes, kitchenware, and cookie jars. The most popular cookie jars are the Smiley pig, Muggsy dog, Puss n' Boots, and Dutch Jack and Jill. My cookie jar was the Dutch Jill.

Now, this is where it gets interesting. The gold-trimmed jars are the most sought after and you will never guess why—not in a million years. They are seconds! Gold and decals were applied to the seconds to hide their imperfections. These jars never made it to the five and dimes, but instead were sold in specialty shops at a higher price. And now they command much higher prices. According to one article I read, "The sky's the limit when it comes to the rarer gold-trimmed, decorated jars."

My cookie jar not only had the gold trim, but also a large applied decal of flowers. Wow! Yikes! Score! I did pay $18 for her, so I started the auction at $24.99

People often mistake Shawnee for a similar type of pottery called McCoy (and vice versa). Production methods can help you identify them correctly. The majority of Shawnee was glazed both inside and out, except for an unglazed raised rim on the bottom of the piece. Some of the larger Shawnee pieces may be completely unglazed on the base, showing the white clay body and mold lines.

McCoy and Shawnee both produced matte (dull) and shiny glazes. Some pieces were decorated with cold paint (paint that is applied after the glaze has been fired). This paint was not durable and could come off easily. Any piece with cold paint should be handled with great care.

Unfortunately, like many of the other American potteries, Shawnee couldn't compete against cheaper pieces made overseas. It closed its doors in 1961. Many of the molds were sold and are still in use, so watch for reproductions. A new Shawnee pottery also started in the 1990s, but its pieces are signed with a very different mark. So watch out! And please watch my 30-minute infomercial when it comes to a television station in your area, and look for this Dutch Jill cookie jar.

#90 Shogun Mikasa Dinner Set

$100.00 Paid
From: Garage sale

1 Dinner Plate Mikasa Shogun A6851 Cinnebar Black RARE

Description:

This is the Shogun pattern by Mikasa A 6851. You are bidding on one 10½" dinner plate. We have a lot of pieces in this pattern up for sale this week in separate auctions. It is an awesome Asian-inspired pattern. Only made from 1978 to 1987 and currently discontinued. Black and cinnabar red panels with white and cinnabar colored flowers. No chips, no cracks, no crazing.

Winning Bid: **$419.76/24**

Ended: 9/22/07
History: 24/24 store listings
Starting Bid: $9.99 to $24.99
Winner: Hesperia, CA

Viewed
 **X**

Shogun Mikasa Dinner Set #90

The Story

I was at an estate sale that my friend was running and the pieces were exquisite. This was a beautiful dinner set with six each of four different items. Six dinners, six salads, six breads and six cup and saucer sets. I would call it a 24-piece set, but as most of you already know, cups and saucers are always counted separately—so it would be considered a 30-piece set.

It didn't matter, because it was priced at $750! I turned over a plate and read "Mikasa." I thought, "Someone is nuts," and I knew it wasn't my friend. Several weeks later at a different sale, there was the same set, but now correctly priced at $100. I asked my friend, "What was that all about?" She said that the owner had put the original price on it, but had finally come to his senses. Thank goodness!

After the Japanese attacked Pearl Harbor in 1941 and the United States entered WWII, the American government forced about 110,000 Japanese-Americans— that is, American citizens of Japanese descent—into internment camps. The fear was that the Japanese were going to make a full-blown attack on our shores, and that Japanese-Americans were likely to be sympathetic to the Japanese invaders rather than the United States. Most of the camps were on the west coast (in Washington, Oregon, and California) on sites such as empty horse racing tracks and fairgrounds. The internment ended on January 2nd, 1945. It was a great tragedy.

The founder of Mikasa, George Aratani, was one of these Japanese-Americans. When he was 24 years old, he was placed in an internment camp near his home of Guadalupe, California, where his father owned a farm. Several years after his release, he decided to visit Japan to look for business ventures.

Originally, he wanted to import tuna, but the freezing facilities in Japan were inadequate. A friend suggested a non-perishable item, and he began importing dinnerware in 1948. The company was called "American Commercial" until 1957, when it changed its name to "Mikasa." It also started manufacturing its own lines: flatware, dinnerware, crystal, and so on.

The "Shogun" pattern I sold was very Japanese in design. "Shogun" is a historical title for a commander in the armed forces of Japan. The word comes from *"sho"* (which means "commander") and *"gun"* (meaning "military troops").

During WWII, times were hard for many people in this country. Food, milk, gasoline, and many other things were rationed. I still have many of my grandparents' ration books. Luckily, my grandfather Elmer was a good hunter and he had a great hunting dog named Britt. He would often bring home pheasant for my grandmother to cook.

Out of tough times come tougher people. George Aratani became a very successful entrepreneur despite his internment, and I was very happy when his "Shogun" dinnerware set made me over $300 from my eBay store.

#91 Waechtersbach Christmas Bowl

25¢
Paid
From: Bellingham charity sale

Waechtersbach Winter Dreams Footed Christmas Bowl 2070

Description:
Footed bowl with a winter theme. Made in West Germany. 5" by 3.5". Blue with white snow scene, gold stars and trim. Darling. Pattern number is 2070. No chips, no cracks, no crazing.

Winning Bid:

$51.⁰⁰

Ended: 9/26/07
History: 8 bids
Starting Bid: $9.99
Winners: Lacey, WA

Viewed

000133 X

Waechtersbach Christmas Bowl #91

The Story

When I was growing up, we moved quite a bit for my dad's work. After living in Monmouth, Oregon, until third grade, we had to move to Olympia, Washington, so that my dad could teach at the high school there. My parents found a house in San Mar Villas in a suburb of Olympia called Lacey. I loved that house at 216 Shadow Circle. I had a bedroom with a private bath and walk-in closet on the lower level. It was sweet, and I was ten years old!

I remember going to antiques shows in Portland with my grandma when we lived in Lacey. I would pack a tiny suitcase and walk to the entrance of our neighborhood, where I would wait for my grandma to drive up. She wouldn't come to the house because we were in a hurry. Can you imagine letting a ten-year-old wait alone on a busy street blocks from home? During one trip, I waited until we were already ten miles away from Lacey before looking at my grandma and saying, "I really don't want to go because I don't want to miss school." She said, "No problem, honey," turned around, and drove me right to my front door. My G was awesome!

I bought this little bowl at a charity sale in Bellingham in the summer while at my mom's beach house. When I buy things while I'm on the road, I usually do a little research before shipping the items home to make sure that they are worth paying the postage. I looked this bowl up on Replacements.com and found nothing listed. I had only paid 25 cents, so thought it was worth shipping back home. Boy, was I right.

It was made by Waechtersbach and featured a neat winter scene with ice skating and snow. The company Waechtersbach (very hard to say and spell) was founded in 1832 by the Prince of Isenburg-Waechtersbach, from whom it gets its name.

Waechtersbach ceramics have a unique brilliance and color that come from the company's special glazes. Waechtersbach pieces have a particular feel that makes them easy to recognize. I love their red ware with the white hearts that was very popular in the 1970s and 1980s.

Back in the 1970s in my little suburb of Olympia, there was a lake which would freeze over in the winter. My best friend Patty Harvey and her sister Rhonda and I would walk to the lake with our ice skates to go skating. Patty's family lived two houses away from ours and they owned a pet store. I have tried to find Patty Harvey on the Internet over the years with no luck. I had better luck with this bowl.

I couldn't believe it when this piece sold to someone in Lacey, Washington. It really brought back memories, and this piece really brought in the "ka-ching"! I guess I am lucky to have lived to adulthood and have such good memories, considering I was left waiting alone on a major highway at age ten and also allowed to go ice skating on a lake with no adult supervision.

Will wonders never cease?

#92 North American Paintings

$2.00/2
Paid
From: Garage sale

Native American Thunderbird Painting Primitive Batdorf
Native American Thunderbird Painting Batdorf Fish Neat

Description:
I bought two of these same type paintings at a very upper-end estate sale in Bellingham, WA. This one is 7.25" by 7". "Carol Batdorf" written in pencil on back. We don't know if she was the owner or the artist. Really neat with a wooden frame. White, red, brick, black, and taupe. Definitely vintage.

Winning Bid: $60.98/2

Ended: 9/29/07
History: 8 bids/2
Starting Bid: $9.99 ea
Winner: Duluth, GA

Viewed

000071 X

North American Paintings   #92

The Story

I bought these paintings, oil on wood, at a very high-end estate sale in Bellingham. There were only $1 each, so figured I couldn't go wrong—AND they would ship very easily back to Palm Desert. I don't bother with research when it comes to small non-breakables!

I described the paintings as "Native American" because that's what they appeared to be. Recently, however, eBay has really cracked down on this. If you cannot prove what tribe or nation an item is from, but you have "Native American" or "NA" in the title, your listings can be shut down. For a while, there was a very strange eBayer who watched all my auctions and store items and would turn me in for the slightest "NA" infraction. Finally, I emailed the person and said, "Get a life!" and they backed off.

Both of these pieces had thunderbirds on them, but no artist signature on the front. "Carol Batdorf" was written on the back of both in pencil, and after doing some research on her, I discovered that she is the author and illustrator of many children's books about Native Americans. So it seems clear that she was the artist.

I grew up loving to read. Luckily, my kids are the same way. My dad, after leaving teaching jobs at major universities, took an administrative job for the school district in Bellingham in 1976 so that we could live close to both sets of grandparents. About four years later, the school district went through a budget cutting cycle and had to eliminate his position.

Instead of moving us again, he took a step down and accepted a librarian position at Fairhaven Middle School. I am proud of my dad for putting his family first. Fairhaven was where my dad went to junior high! No wonder we all love to read. And I bet he ordered Carol Batdorf's books for his library!

The thunderbird is a legendary creature in Native American history and traditions—a supernatural bird of power and strength. It is a very important part of Pacific Northwest culture and appears frequently in Pacific Coast art, songs, and histories. The thunderbird is thought to be intelligent, powerful—and vindictive. If you make a thunderbird angry, it will get revenge.

The thunderbird gets its name from the belief that the beating of its enormous wings causes thunder and windstorms. Boy, do we get windstorms here in Palm Desert. And boy, did we get thunder and wind storms in Bellingham.

I was very pleased when these two pieces sold for over $60. I am also proud of my dad who was (and is) intelligent and strong. He did a great job raising us with my mom (of course) and I will always be grateful to him for all his belief in me. I remember in 1994, when I had my idea for a line of greeting cards. I ran over to see him in his office at the Fairhaven library. I was excited as I showed him my prototypes, and he said, "Go for it." He never stops believing in me or supporting me, even when he thinks I am crazy! And he probably thinks that a lot!

#93 Antique Elf Golf Mugs

$2.⁰⁰/2
Paid
From: Garage sale in Rancho Mirage

Antique Golfing Victorian Beer Stein Mug Transfer Ware
Antique Golfer Green Beer Mug Stein Victorian Elf Golf

Description:

Antique golfing beer mug is 4¼" tall. Paint or transfer is worn. 2" crack. No maker's marks. The antique golfers are so neat. Even in "as is" condition—still a great piece. I would guess 1900s to 1930s. Maybe earlier. This one has a lady in long skirt on the front side.

This antique beer mug or coffee mug has characters on it that resemble elves. 4¼" tall. Wear to pattern. 3" brown crack. No maker's marks. The Victorian golfers are so neat. This one has a man on the front side. 1900s to 1930s and maybe earlier.

Winning Bid:

$59.⁵⁴/2

Ended: 10/5/07
History: 4 bids/2
Starting Bid: $9.99 ea
Winner: UK and MI

Viewed

001649 **X**

The Story

I had spent some time with Skip and Karen McGrath (eBay gurus) at eBay Live in Boston. Skip was putting together a boot camp in Anacortes, Washington, in September and he asked me if I would like to teach. Sure, why not? What was one more trip in the most travel-packed year of my life? But being so close to Bellingham would give me a chance to see my dad, sister, and nephew.

I was only able to see my dad for about five minutes, but I got to spend quality time with my sister Kiki and her baby Zach. Skip and his wife Karen were kind enough to invite them to the opening evening party for the boot camp, and we had a great time.

The boot camp went well and it was filmed by my good friend John Mortensen. His wife Audrey worked for me in the antiques store forever. She was my first employee! And our kids were born just a few months apart.

While I was teaching, I got this email asking if I would end these two auctions early with a "Buy It Now":

"Hi—I have a couple of plates with the same transferware designs— a variety of men & women golfers and caddies. Guessing they might be worth about $50 each, given the condition. Would you take $100 for them both right now? Thanks."

I never end auctions early. I don't care how much a prospective buyer offers, I have never done it, because asking a seller to end an auction early is a tactic some buyers use if they suspect the auction will go high. These pieces were quite damaged, however, and I had sold

something similar about six months earlier which didn't sell for much. So I posed the question to our students: "What do you all think?"

Well, my friend John (our cameraman) yelled from the back of the room, "Are you crazy? Just do it. You only paid $2." Carol, a student, suggested we check to see what the person who made the offer had been buying on eBay. Brilliant! We found that this eBayer had been buying quite a lot of transferware golfing pieces, and that some were selling in the $500 range. So he had a lot of knowledge about transferware, and he seemed to be able to afford expensive pieces.

Transferware was invented in the 1750s in England. The process starts with an engraved copper plate. This plate is used to print a pattern in ink on tissue paper; the tissue paper is then applied to a ceramic surface and the ceramic is fired at a low temperature to fix the pattern. This process saves hours of hand painting.

I decided to stick with my policy and emailed the eBayer to let him know. I ended the email by saying, "You may even get them for a lot less than you offered. Good luck!" As it turned out, the winners of the auctions did get them for less than the eBayer's offer. I left $40.46 on the table. I guess there's an exception to every rule!

#94 Madame Alexander Dolls

$4.⁰⁰/2 Paid

From: Garage sale in Anacortes, WA

Wizard of Oz Munchkin Peasant Doll Madame Alexander HTF Wizard of Oz Mayor Munchkinland Madame Alexander Doll

Description:

This girl doll has the original MA tag and a price tag from Neiman Marcus. 10½" tall with hat. In very good condition. Needs slight cleaning.

This boy doll is 8½" tall and still has his original MA tag. The hat may be faded but otherwise in very good condition. Needs slight cleaning.

Winning Bid:

$80.⁸⁶/2

Ended: 10/7/07
History: 17 bids/2
Starting Bid: $9.99
Winner: Georgia

Viewed

 **X**

Madame Alexander Dolls #94

The Story

I was usually passing through Anacortes in a rush on my way to catch a ferry to the San Juan Islands. While teaching at the boot camp, I got to take the students to actual Anacortes garage sales and see what a cute town it is. Karen, Cindy, Judy, Leon, Mike, Robin, Carol, George, and Chris—along with our cameraman John—all piled into three vehicles and off we went.

What should have been a short drive became quite the adventure, because I was leading and made a few wrong turns—including an illegal left turn. We finally made it to the first sale after many detours. At that sale, I was able to buy some amazing Wizard of Oz items that most of the students thought were just junk.

I had been very careful that morning at breakfast to tell all the students not to mention eBay at any garage sales. Sellers do not respond well to that information. I think it just makes them worry about the money they're losing by not selling on eBay themselves. So if anyone ever asks why you are buying so much, I recommend that you be as vague as you can without lying.

Completely forgetting my warning, one of my favorite students from the boot camp (and I won't mention any names because I promised not to) announced to the folks at the Wizard of Oz garage sale, "Lynn is an eBay seller." Immediate silence.

Despite the awkwardness that followed, I managed to purchase these two darling Madame Alexander dolls for $2 each. Madame Alexander ("MA") was founded around 1929 by Beatrice Alex-

ander. Beatrice was the daughter of Russian immigrants and was raised in the apartment above her father's doll hospital—the first doll hospital in America. A doll hospital is just what it sounds like—a toy shop devoted to doll repair. How cool is that?

Beatrice often played with the dolls, and her love of this pastime inspired her to create her own line. Her dolls are fine quality and handcrafted. You can often tell an MA doll before you even pick it up.

Beatrice created the first collectible dolls based on a licensed character—Scarlett O'Hara from *Gone with the Wind*. Gund also claims to be the first company to use licensed characters. I guess both companies can have this distinction since production of these toys was happening at the same time. Madame Alexander is still in business today, although it was bought out in 1995 by a limited partnership.

My $4 investment turned into over $80. Pretty cool! I seem to be selling a lot of dolls lately. This may be because when I was growing up, not only was I called "the Dralle dolly," but all three of us kids, on occasion, were called "the Dralle dollies." Check us out in these wild mod outfits that my mother made! I bet those would fetch a pretty penny on eBay today.

#95 Fabienne Jouvin Ginger Jar

$30.⁰⁰
Paid
From: Garage sale

French Cloisonné Ginger Jar Fabienne Jouvin Paris Super

Description:
Signed vase or ginger jar with lid. 5½" by 5½" and in excellent condition. Signed "Fabienne Jouvin Paris." Off white/ivory, black, and orange. Very well-known and expensive French designer France.

Winning Bid:

$105.⁴⁹

Ended: 10/14/07
History: 15 bids
Starting Bid: $24.99
Winners: NC

Viewed
 X

Fabienne Jouvin Ginger Jar #95

The Story

When I used to tell people in Bellingham that I ran my grandmother's antiques store, invariably they would say something like, "Oh, that place on Northwest with all the bottles in the windows." "No, those are antiques in the window, and we sell much more than bottles," I would say. Eventually, Audrey and I took down the shelves that you see to the right of my grandmother in the photo and made that space into a display window that we constantly changed and updated.

Spending time on the display window really improved our walk-in traffic. It was true—my grandmother had so many more interesting things than just those items in the window. She loved cloisonné and had a stockpile in the snake pit (which was the jam-packed storage room off of her old bedroom). I still remember her good friend (and one of her best customers) Joanne Peters. She loved green cloisonné, and for every special event, her husband Clarence would come to the shop and ask my grandma to pull out a treasure from the snake pit so he could take it home for Joanne.

I am sure Joanne has one of the most amazing collections around. Cloisonné is made by a very painstaking process that involves shaping wire into intricate patterns, and then applying layer after layer of enamel into the spaces framed by the wires. The elaborate process of creating cloisonné was invented in the near east (between the Mediterranean and what is now Iran), then spread to the Byzantine Empire (Rome in the Middle Ages), and from there along the Silk Road (the trade routes from Europe) to China.

I picked up this amazing piece on the ground at a garage sale and found it was marked $40. I told the seller I thought it was just beautiful but a little more than I could spend. She let me have it for $30.

I had never seen cloisonné signed "France." The artist, Fabienne Jouvin, designs for quite a few high-end stores including Gumps. She not only does the enamel ware, but also works in ceramics. Her dinnerware patterns are stunning! Her "Thousand Fires" pattern sells for $800 per 24-piece set. That is $33.33 a piece. I would like to find a box full of her china at a garage sale for sure!

Fabienne's designs are wonderful, as she fuses western and eastern cultures in a style that is uniquely her own. Fabienne roamed the world from China to Cuba (kind of like cloisonné), and her passion in design comes from mixing different cultural elements.

I had to have this box, even though it was $30. I started it at $24.99 and was very happy when it sold for over $100 and went to North Carolina.

I have to tell you, sometimes when I was working at the antique shop, I felt like I was putting out a thousand fires a day. That place was fun and yet so hectic—there was always something that needed my attention. I miss it and I miss my grandmother.

#96 Pink Poodle Sign

$3.^{00}
Paid
From: Garage sale

Big Pink Poodle Store Display Sign Lucite Darling Fun

Description:
Hot "Pink Poodle" store display sign is darling. Quite large. 12" by 30". Was from a store display for the brand "Pink Poodle." Has two holes for hanging and in very good condition.

Winning Bid: $110.^{27}

Ended: 10/18/07
History: 14 bids
Starting Bid: $9.99
Winner: Los Angeles, CA

Viewed
 X

Pink Poodle Sign #96

The Story

I was at a garage sale where all the items were samples from a company called "Pink Poodle." I had never heard of it, but the clothes were darling and only $1 each. They were so cheap because most of them had a small cut in the middle back. I was told that the cuts had been made deliberately so that they would not be charged as real merchandise when going through customs. I bought a huge bunch of clothes because I knew that Indy or I would wear them or I could sell them on eBay.

Mind you, this was back when my little princess wanted to dress like a princess and wear only big, pink, elaborate dresses. Check out the big poofy pink ball gown she wore for preschool graduation...it was too cute. Her best friend Paige looks darling in her daisy dress, but Indy wanted to make a statement, and of course Houston had to get into the act. Check out his googly eyes. I love this photo!

As I was leaving the sale, I spotted a large Lucite sign that said "Pink Poodle." It was $3. I thought it would be darling in Indy's pink room, so I bought it. Well, when I got home and showed it to her, she said, "Not so much." That means, "I don't want it."

I am soooo glad she didn't like it! I couldn't believe it when it sold for over $110! I kept some of the clothes from that sale, and Indy took a few shirts, but I listed the rest and they have been selling slowly but surely.

I think the sign sold for so much because pink is so popular and poodle owners really love their breed. I just read an article about a woman being fined $1,000 for dyeing her poodle pink. Yikes!

The poodle is known as one of the most intelligent breeds of dog. And I thought poodles were just pretty! The poodle was originally bred as a water dog for hunting, but is now considered a non-sporting variety.

Poodles originated in Germany, and the poodle clip—the classic poodle haircut, which seems to be all about fashion rather than function—was originally designed to protect the dogs' vital organs and joints, yet let them move quickly through water.

The French are responsible for turning the poodle from a sporting dog into a non-sporting dog. They also developed the different poodle sizes (toy through standard) through breeding.

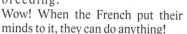

Wow! When the French put their minds to it, they can do anything!

My head is spinning from all this poodle history. I just know that my kids want a dog and at this point in our lives, it is not even an option. We are gone almost every weekend, and spending a lot of time in a kennel would not be fair to a sweet little puppy. But I think I have been more than fair to my kids in their upbringing. They have a mom who ALWAYS puts them first and is ALWAYS there for their most important moments.

#97 Mottahedeh Covered Vegetable

33¢
Paid
From: Estate sale

Fruits of the Sea Soup Tureen Mottahedeh Oval Vegetable

Description:
This is an amazing piece that needs some TLC. It is either a soup tureen or an oval covered vegetable serving bowl. Most likely a vegetable serving bowl because there is no hole for a ladle. However it is huge!! Signed on the base "Fruits of the Sea Portugal A Mottahedah Design." Does have some repair needs. There is no knob on the top and one of the handles needs repair. 9" by 14" by 8½". Coimbra Portugal. Also signed with "5-2006." A very hard-to-find piece and rare with figural shell handles.

Winning Bid:

$24.⁹⁹

Ended: 10/19/07
History: 2 bids
Starting Bid: $24.99
Winner: Winchester, VA

Viewed

000716 X

Mottahedeh Covered Vegetable #97

The Story

Peter and I were on Catalina Island scuba diving while this ocean-inspired vegetable dish was selling. Catalina is just off the coast of Los Angeles and is an amazing area with about 4,000 residents.

After a history of Native Americans inhabiting the island, it became a home for Russian otter hunters, Yankee smugglers, and fishermen. During the 1800s, many people tried to develop it into a resort destination. The first Catalina hotel, the Hotel Metropole, was built in 1887 (and was coincidentally where Peter and I stayed). It has been redone and is very nice.

The island changed hands many times and was finally bought out completely by chewing gum magnate William Wrigley, Jr. in 1919. From 1927 to 1937, pottery and tiles were made on the island at the Catalina Clay products company. Watch for these pieces, because they sell for a lot. The Chicago Cubs (owned by Wrigley) used the island for spring training from 1921 to 1951. How cool is that? In 1975, Philip Wrigley deeded Santa Catalina Island to the Conservancy, which now protects 88% of the island.

The round Casino at Catalina, in front of which we all scuba dive, was built in 1929 by Wrigley as a dance hall. The name "Casino" was meant to suggest a social gathering place; the Casino has never served as a gambling hall. When it was built, it was hailed as a two-million-dollar palace of pleasure. It is the only building of its size in the world built on a fully circular plan. A huge motion picture theater is on the ground floor, and it still shows movies. Above is the world's largest circular ballroom. For some reason, this all reminds me of the Rotunda from story #35.

Mottahedeh has been in business since 1934 (about the time the Casino was built!), and it makes classical decorative accessories and tableware. The company's expensive patterns are based on early European and Chinese designs. Mottahedeh has licenses to reproduce designs from the Metropolitan Museum of Art, Colonial Williamsburg, and Monticello. They have made china for the President and the State Department.

Mottahedeh is based in New York, and what I love about their items is that they are made in very elegant shapes, vibrant colors, and are hand-painted. The best part of all? Everything they make has a story, just like everything in this book has some type of story!

The lady who bought this piece sent an email: "Hi Lynn. I do professional restoration of porcelain and I want to sell the repaired pieces on eBay. I am a nut for Mottahedeh! Linda."

Now I am a nut for Mottahedeh. I had never heard of it until I bought this for 33 cents. If it had been in perfect condition, it would have been worth $415.95 on Replacements. I started this piece at $24.99 because I knew that in "as is" condition it would take a special buyer like Linda. I loved the crab, shrimp, oysters, lobster, and shells that adorned this piece. All the sea life we saw that weekend on Catalina may have been what inspired the Mottahedeh designers.

#98 Playmobil Vintage Sets

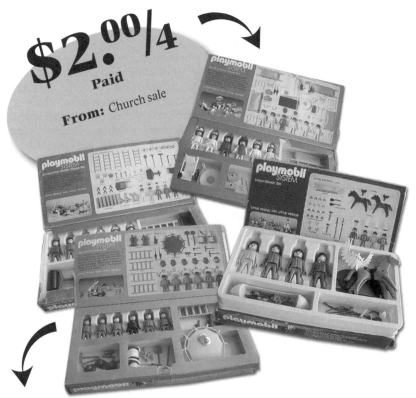

$2.00/4
Paid
From: Church sale

Playmobil Schafer Fire Fighters Deluxe Set #70 Vintage

Description:
Great Playmobil Fire Fighter set. The pieces are in very good to excellent condition. There is some wear to two of the fireman's faces—I think that black ink could fix these. It is missing 1 walkie talkie, 1 nozzle and 2 smoke masks (nothing major). Everything else is there. The box is in very "as is" condition—it has been taped shut with brown packing tape. We have several vintage sets up for sale this week in separate auctions.

Winning Bid:

$54.70/4
Ended: 11/10/07
History: 19 bids/4
Starting Bid: $9.99 ea auction
Winner: MN and France

Viewed

001372 X

Playmobil Vintage Sets #98

The Story

When we used to go to my Great-grandma Sussex's house on Sundays, everyone would sit around and play cards. My grandma loved cards, also, and I would often find her playing solitaire on her coffee table when I would arrive at the shop. It is funny, but after I finish each story in this book, I treat myself to one spider solitaire game. Spider solitaire is a very addictive computer game, and playing it is my little reward to myself.

Toys and games are very good sellers on eBay. One popular brand of kids' toys is Playmobil, which I learned about from Mo. When she started selling for herself on eBay, one of the first things she sold was a Playmobil set that her son had never opened. It brought in over $40! She mentioned it to me in passing about three years ago, but I never gave it a second thought... until I was at a church sale and I saw four boxes (completely beat up and taped shut) marked "Playmobil." "Ding! Ding! Ding!" An alarm went off in my mind. I paid 50 cents each and bought them all.

As soon as I got home, I started doing some research. Yikes! In perfect condition, the cowboy and Indian set would sell for about $67. Mine was far from perfect, but was only missing a few items on the inside. I decided to find out more about the company.

Playmobil, sometimes just called "Playmo," is a line of toys made by the Brandstatter Group out of Zirndorf, Germany. The company was started in 1876 by a locksmith named Andreas Brandstatter who specialized in lock and metal fittings. In 1908, his son George took over, and by the 1930s the company was making telephones, cash registers, and various metal items for toy shops.

In 1958, when the hula hoop craze hit, George's son Horst invented a machine that could mold soft plastic hoses into hoops. The company made a fortune manufacturing hula hoops. Horst's technique allowed him to make toys in any shape, and soon a prototype for the first Playmobil set was invented with the help of Hans Beck.

Hans Beck is considered "The Father of Playmobil." His toy designs were simple and flexible—great for kids. The faces of the Playmobil figures were based on children's drawings (large heads, big smiles and no noses). The first Playmobil sets were sold worldwide in 1975. I think my charity sale finds were some of the earliest sets, because they had "1976" on the boxes!

The first construction worker set included workers' accessories as well as three crates of the German national drink: beer. This set's packaging caused an uproar, as it showed two of the figures discussing their beer drinking. "That's my fifth bottle today," said one of the figures. "Don't worry, we've got enough beer" replied another. You can imagine some parents' reactions to these toys. Unfortunately, that is NOT the construction set I got—because I bet it is worth a small fortune today!

I was thrilled when these four sets sold for almost $55 and went off to France. The firefighter set sold for the most, at $20.50. Thanks, Mo!

#99 Meriden Tea Pot Set

$150.⁰⁰/4

Paid

From: Estate sale

Repousse Meriden Britannia 1934 Tea Pot Insects Antique

Description:

This is an amazing tea pot. "1934" and "5" on the base. It rocks a little bit. There is a bird on a branch, a dragonfly, and a sunflower. 10½" and 6" tall. We have quite a few pieces up for sale in this pattern. It is Meriden Britannia and they are all signed with "Meriden Quadruple Silverplate." Made in USA. Antique. Silverplate is in perfect condition. Hand hammered finish. Beautiful. Raised design. Please check out our other pieces that we have up for sale in separate auctions.

Winning Bid:

$580.³⁰/4

Ended: 11/9/07
History: 30 bids/4
Starting Bid: $49.99 ea auction
Winner: Studio City, CA

Viewed

 X

Meriden Tea Pot Set   #99

The Story

When an item is signed "quadruple plate," that means it has four times the usual amount of silver plating. My best guy friend in college was also a "quadruple." He was William John Payes IV, and we called him Jay. I also called him "Jota," which is the letter "J" in Spanish. We had so much fun when we were together at USC, and we talked almost every day when I was in Spain for my semester abroad. I missed him so much that when my dad was buying my plane ticket home from Madrid, he scheduled a stopover in Chicago so that I could spend some time with Jay before heading home.

Jay's family was very proper and wealthy. I was actually invited out for tea at a fancy country club with his family when I was there. I was a little intimidated, but we ended up having a lovely time. This tea set reminded me of that experience.

I found this set at an estate sale and paid $150 for it. It was very beautiful, with insects all over it done in the repousse style. *"Repousse"* is a French word that means "pushed up" and is a metalworking technique in which a metal piece is shaped by hammering from the reverse side.

The Meriden Brittania Company was formed in 1852 in Meriden, Connecticut. Its store at Union Square was an amazing place. It had a tradition during the nineteenth century of taking its wares out of their usual closed cases at Christmas (Jay's birthday) and setting them out to allow customers to handle them.

In 1898, Meriden Brittania convinced fourteen independent silver companies from the Meriden area to come together to form the International Silver Company. The member companies kept their identities and continued to mark silverware with their own signatures. In addition, International had its own mark that was used on products made by the parent company. They are still in business today.

This beautiful tea set came with four pieces, a sugar bowl, a tea pot, a creamer, and a waste bowl. A waste bowl was originally used in a regular table service to allow diners to remove unwanted food from their plates. The waste bowl was incorporated into the standard tea set around 1750, where its purpose was to allow a tea drinker to pour out cold tea left in the cup before getting a new warm cup.

The tea pot ended up selling for the most, at $218.26. I was thrilled when my $150 investment turned into almost $600 in one week. That was something to write home about—or at least write about in this book.

Jay wrote me lots of letters over the years, and he always signed them, "I love you, as always." He passed away ten years ago at the age of thirty-five. It was very hard to lose a friend who loved me unconditionally and was always there to pick me up if I needed it (literally and figuratively). I have never wanted to write a story about Jay because I knew it would be so sad. But he was a huge part of my life. As always.

#100 Cherub Angel Pitcher

$0.00 Paid

From: Inheritance

Cranberry Mary Gregory Pitcher Cherub Angel Antique Art

Description:
This is a beautiful antique pitcher. 7" by 5". This amazing piece was one of my grandmother's favorites. It now belongs to my mom, and she has decided to part with it so I am selling it for her. There is some gold wear, but no chips, no cracks, no crazing. Rough pontil. Hand blown and I am guessing English 1870s to 1880s. Victorian jug, pitcher, or ewer. Applied clear glass handle. White with gold leaves in a Webb style. Also painted in the style of Mary Gregory who made the white applied children designs. A treasure!

Winning Bid:

$450.00

Ended: 11/17/07
History: 1 bid (sold in store)
Starting Bid: $499.00
Winner: Salamanca, NY

Viewed

001576 X

Cherub Angel Pitcher #100

The Story

It just seems so fitting to end this book with a story about one of my grandmother's favorite pieces. As you may already know, my grandmother collected cranberry glass, and her kitchen shelves were jam-packed with this beautiful reddish-pink glass. She had brought many pieces over from England, because that is where most antique cranberry was produced.

This was one of her favorites because it had a cherub or angel on it. In addition to collecting cranberry, my grandmother also collected cherubs, due to the fact that when she was little, people thought she looked like a cherub with her big cheeks. I have one photo of her in which she looks just like a little angel. Unfortunately, we have all inherited those chubby little cheeks. And they don't look so great on adults.

In addition to the cheeks, my mom also inherited this piece. As we are all trying to downsize, she decided she would sell it. I told her I would list it for her. We started the bidding at $499. No takers. So we moved it into my eBay store with a "Make Offer" option. I love this feature on eBay because it can't hurt to entertain offers, and half the time people pay the full price anyway and don't even bother to make an offer.

About six months after we got this listed, we got an offer for $450. I said, "Take it!" That is a lot of money for an item that could get broken. You may be wondering why it sold for so much, so I am going to tell you.

Cranberry glass is also called "gold ruby" in Europe. It is not a dark red color, but more of a pinkish-red shade that is made by adding real gold to the molten glass during the glassmaking process. Due to the high cost of gold, this glass is never mass produced, but is instead hand blown or molded into individual pieces.

The process for making cranberry glass was discovered in either Bohemia or Italy in the seventeenth century. The most famous period of production was in the 1800s in England, and this is the date range for most of the pieces my grandmother owned.

And even better, this piece had a white angel painted on it in the Mary Gregory style. Mary Gregory was born in 1856 and died in 1908; she was a glass painter at the Boston and Sandwich Glass Company on Cape Cod in Massachusetts. She became very well known for painting Victorian-era children with a white enamel paint that would be fired onto the glass.

Most Mary Gregory pieces (as we call them today) were not, in fact, painted by Mary. In the 1920s, artists and companies who noticed the popularity of Mary Gregory's work began producing pieces that resembled hers. Over time, her name became the generic term for this style. Fenton is quite famous for making a lot of Mary Gregory style items.

This was one of my grandmother's favorite pieces, and my grandmother was one of my very favorite people.

Afterword

I shed a lot of tears writing these books. The memories that each story bring back are amazing. Some are happy memories, some really sad, and some just make me wistful. Most of them make me miss my grandmother. Although it has been almost nine years since she passed away, I dream about her a lot.

One dream I keep having is that I have to get everything in her house packed up and put away so the new owners can move in. It seems like once a week I am packing up my grandmother's personal items. I think I have this dream because I didn't finish the job of emptying out the house.

My dad did it for me. It was over Christmas break in 2002 after we had already moved to California. We (me, Houston and Indy) came up and did what we could with my mom's and sister's help, but had to leave without completely emptying out the house

Honestly, I don't think I could have done it. It would have been too sad to lock that back door for the last time. My grandmother lived in that house for over 50 years. And I am very attached to that house. In fact, I still carry the two keys to her back door with me on my keychain.

I also tend to cry a lot when I spend hours and hours going through old photos to find the perfect side photo for a story. And then sometimes, I am overjoyed when I do find that perfect photo. The photo for story #46—of Houston with USC football coach Pete Carroll—took me four weeks to locate. I was thrilled when I found it.

I was supposed to get a photo of the new owner of the Harley bags for story #19 with his motorcycle and he never sent it. At the last minute, I found a photo of my grandmother sitting on a motorcycle in the 1920s! How amazing is that?

Thank you so much for reading my books! They are seriously labors of love and I try to put as much useful eBay information in them as I can while still making the stories entertaining. I hope I succeeded.

Please sign up for my free newsletter (ezine) at www.TheQueenofAuctions.com. It is full of fun tips, tricks, and more stories every two weeks.

I do appreciate all of you who write to us and send us your stories. We are still working on *The 100 Best Things You All Have Sold on eBay,* so if you have a story, please email it to Stories@TheQueenofAuctions.com.

Maybe by showing you the keys to my grandma's back door, it will close it for me.

God bless you and Godspeed.

Sign up for Lynn's free twice-a-month newsletter!
It's a Home Run!

Lynn's electronic newsletter (ezine) will be delivered every other Thursday right to your email inbox. Sign up now at **www.TheQueenofAuctions.com**

Lynn's ezine is chock full of great eBay stories and tips to help grow *your* eBay business. Sign up today!

TheQueenofAuctions.com

See what readers have to say:

I have been devouring Lynn's FREE newsletters and have learned more about having your own online business from her than I did from all of the ebooks I've spent hundreds of dollars on in the last 10 years. -Jackie Farri

I read one of Lynn's books and went from having a $1,200 a year eBay business to over $10,000 a year eBay business. Her free ezine has taught me the ropes. What an encouragement she is. -Denise, Pennsylvania

Lynn is an inspiration to us all. Her Queen's Court, ezines, teleseminars, and DVDs have helped me to get to where I am and give me hope for a bright future. Thanks, Lynn, for everything! -Jude (a Queen's Court Member)

Lynn is my guru and my inspiration. She has helped me (and many, many others) tremendously through her work, her books, her CDs, and her ezine. -Anita Sharpe

Lynn is very inspiring. After reading many ezines and ordering her Boot Camp in a Box, I have quit my JOB and do eBay full time. In three months I have made more money than I did last year working for eight months. -Sherry

If you would like to experience Lynn's Live Boot Camp from the comfort of your home, please check out her Boot Camp in a Box at **www.BootCampBox.com**

Use these blank pages to record your own **Home Runs** !